Waking up from the American Dream

Book II:
MAKING IT HOME

MICHELE MAINGOT CABRAL

Other books in the series:

Waking up from the American Dream
Book I: Walking Away

Customer Reviews on Amazon.com:

"Reader beware, be bold as you take this journey with Michele and Mike.
Dare to go slowly, mindfully and introspectively as you trek long the path.
You will explore freedom of choice, personal challenge, self-
empowerment and self-sufficiency. You will consider the importance of
connectedness, simplifying, balance, and place in life. As you get closer to
the Cabral cabin in the woods you will embrace human capacity for hard
work, creativity and spirituality."

-Rosemarie Laurent

"[*Walking* Away] reflects a genuine reverence for nature and a concomitant
call to good stewardship. Featured characters include the author's constant
companions, Hermes, her guiding light Orion's Sirius, hot pickled
milkweed (naturally), random Mormons and ubiquitous black-flies."

-Giovanna

Nice to see someone share what it is like to start out in Maine with
nothing but the love of what's around them and make it work for them.

-Lee Goggin

Cover photo: William West, Milo, Maine

To my two daughters, as you write your own stories upon the pages of the world. Each breath you take is another letter in the story: no more, no less.

CONTENTS

ACKNOWLEDGEMENTS

My heartfelt thanks goes out to my family and friends (especially those who don't like being mentioned for allowing me to use their initials), and all of those who are mentioned in my books. My story would be blank pages without you and I am grateful. I am also eternally grateful to the folks who read and critique my work before publication: Kathy Doore, Consuelo Maingot, Jennifer Sanders, Kent Black, and Karen Starks. I would also like to gratefully acknowledge William West of Milo, Maine, for his cover photograph. I also thank all of my teachers, students, and supporters for encouraging me to continue learning.

Of course, I can't forget Mike, the not-so-silent coauthor of these books, who lovingly nudges me to be a better person.

A FORAGER'S CODE OF ETHICS

1. Only take 1/3 of any plant or group of plants.
2. Always harvest from the outer branches or leaves as you would when pruning.
3. Don't eat all of a plant's seeds. If you harvest mushrooms, brush them off to leave spores.
4. Always ask permission from landowners.
5. When people tell you about a spot they forage, don't tell others.
6. Be respectful and thankful, offering something you value in return. (Native Americans use tobacco and cornmeal, but it could be a prayer, a few deep breaths, or just make time to take it all in.)
7. Forage for what you can use or for what someone you know needs. Avoid an attitude of consumerism. It can lead to overharvesting.
8. Remember that all beings have their seasons. If a species is scarce, let it replenish itself.
9. All beings give. Remember to give.

PROLOGUE
April 3, 2015

We were in the car together on the way to work. Mike was putting in a day at the local flooring establishment to straighten up the showroom. I was on my way to the school to sub for the day.

"I have this tiny nagging anxiety since I published *Walking Away* that people are judging me," I said.

Mike answered in his usual lighthearted but sensitive way, "Stop yur whining! Nobody is judging you!"

I know it, but sometimes I doubt it. My silence spoke the words I was thinking: *but I'm still unsure.*

Mike's tone softened, "Your words are like those little fluffy milkweed seeds. They burst forth and now are just scattered about in every direction. Some will land and plant themselves. Some will not. You have no control over where they're going and who they will touch."

This is why I love Mike so much. He tells it like it is and then he'll bust out with the most insightful poem, his eyes a little damp, and heart swelling. Then he'll follow it up with spilling his greasy breakfast sandwich down the front of the only unstained sweatshirt he owns. How can you resist someone like that?

"Wow, that is so true and so beautifully put. You're right. These words that I formed, polished, and placed in a sleek little package aren't mine. Maybe they never were. They belong to those who read them."

I am no more in charge of them than the milkweed plant is in charge of the silky white seeds it houses in its alien-looking pods.

"From now on, when you feel the nervousness of that thought, just think of those white, fluffy seeds floating in the air sending out good wishes. You'll be fine," he assured me.

And I am.

1. COURAGE
February 20, 2013

I had a strange feeling of disembodiment when I published *Walking Away*. I have been a journal-writer my entire life but never shared my books with anyone. In fact, much of what I have stored in the pages of my little notebooks are things I never even read to myself. It's as though the writing of it was all that was needed at the time. Uncensored, unapologetic, unscripted as they are, these little notes sit in a plastic bin in the basement awaiting what…I don't know.

So I ask myself why I felt compelled to share my journals of the last couple of years in such a public way. If I had known how vulnerable it would make me feel the first couple of months to know that my heart and soul were sitting in the hands of some stranger, open to whatever, I might not have published the book. At one point recently, my adrenaline pumped uncontrollably and I thought I should reverse the whole flow and retract the book. Few people would notice.

That is when I took some time to control my breathing and listened to that slow and steady song of my heart.

What I put out to the world is my truth and my love. This is what my heart song tells me to do. It is the song of courage, teaching me that my truth is the most powerful thing I own and it is my gift to share. Everything gives.

The voice of the feeble mind mentions the fact that I am no expert at any one of the things I mention in the book. True. Each one of us must find the way to the source of our own truths. Like the creative cook, tweaking recipes to suit what works, the songs we each sing along the journey will always be to the rhythm of our own heartbeats.

And so, I listen to mine. My words flow from me as I listen and search for the source. Some days I don't feel courageous enough to share what I find when I get there. These pages are gifts. The words, most sacred to me, are the most precious things I have to give.

I sing the song of my heart here, hoping that those who read will seek to listen to their own songs. Truly, we learn that we can never live vicariously through others' experiences. We need no translators. That is not living.

When we cower, we avoid living; awaiting permission to do something we would like to do. We don't need anyone's permission to feel fully alive. There is no need to wait until we have done this or that before we can awaken from the common dream, listen to the song of our hearts, and start to feel free.

When friends come to visit, we discuss how everyone processes life differently. Some wouldn't think of shopping at Walmart. I do. I understand their reason for refraining from the choice. I understand my reason for making that choice. I don't need anyone's approval.

Tonight I will be hosting a reading from my book to some people in my town at the library. For the first time in a while, I look at my hair. My roots are showing. I think about how I used to spend over a hundred dollars on my hair at least four times a year to look "presentable" at work. Now, I can't afford $15. I think, it takes courage to let yourself go grey. But, tonight, I'm okay with it. My age is a gift too. I have earned this grey hair.

I'm okay with the vulnerability because within the twists and turns of what I can and can't do, is who I truly am and what I have to say. It is the ability to face the source of all things and be confident that I am a part of it.

I recently read an article by Arthur Haines about the nagging realization which we all have that mankind is committing ecocide and that the path to recovering our connection to nature is through foraging.

It is true that when you forage, even just a little, you begin to feel that you are back on the path to that connectedness. You begin to see nature as a place of abundance and joy, the way that children do. You begin to realize that the idea of scarcity and "resources" is a manmade idea that is based on a feeling of separateness.

When people ask me about foraging, I say, just begin with one thing. Look at your own little spot of dirt and allow it to speak to you. Don't tell it, "Well, here you are going to grow daffodils and nothing else this spring." Why kill the wildflowers? Ultimately, they are more valuable and don't require anyone's permission to grow. Even in spite of our attempt to clean them out, they persist.

It amazes me how courageous a simple dandelion is. Maybe that's where it gets its name. It's no wonder that the leaves of this common plant are so good for your heart. Even though we trample upon it, poison it, pull it out by its roots, and generally just give it hell-to-pay, it pops up every spring with its cheerful little smile inviting us to change our minds.

That's how all of nature is. The whole planet is just waiting for man to turn around and gaze upon its beauty and say frankly and honestly, "Wow, thank you for having enough faith in me that eventually I would get it. Thank you for popping back year after year, waving your brightly-colored flags made of butterfly wings, trying desperately to get our attention."

Some humans never lost this connection but they are treated the same way nature has been treated by the rest. It takes a lot of courage for some of these tribes to still practice their connectivity. They hang on in spite of the power struggles. Like the dandelion, they know that someday we will come to our senses and will see the wisdom of their ways.

And yet, there is no one way to get there. We each make the journey according to our rhythms. We can't do it any other way.

Mike and I did a presentation at our local agricultural fair recently. A farmer in the little crowd asked, "Why would I want to eat milkweed? It's the bane of my existence!"

My answer was simple. I told him that if you approach your problem as a solution, you might start to see how the milkweed attracts pollinators. I also said, "What better way to control weeds than to eat their seeds?!" He had to agree and we all laughed. On a more serious note, I explained that, as beekeepers, we would much rather farmers not use weed-killers. "Call *us* the next time you want to get rid of your milkweed," I added.

After reading *Walking Away,* a friend wrote to tell me that he appreciates my viewpoint but is not ready for the leap. He is too comfortable, he said, and he realizes that it is cold out there. My answer is, you don't have to be cold to get it.

You can still wear your three-piece suits to work and send your shirts out to be dry-cleaned.

Just be sure it is the song of your heart that inspires you to do this dance. Take a moment for yourself when no one is looking and pay attention. Notice the steady rhythm of that drum inside you. You are alive. You are a gift. You belong. And, so does everything else.

Your pulse is the same pulse as the river; your blood is the same make-up of the rock, and you can hear the same whispers of wisdom that the wise ones hear. The only difference is that they seek the quiet.

The journey of turning away from the Garden is riddled with ego, separateness, anxiety, and shame. We don't understand why we awaken at three in the morning and can't go back to sleep. Something doesn't feel right. Our brains fill in the blanks with its comfort food: *got to get this done, not enough money, can't forget, what if...*

I don't need to tell you. You take a pill but the dialog comes back. It's like the dandelion with its cheerful smile. It is telling you that you need some time to sit alone or with someone you love and just listen to the song of your own heart. It takes time to hear it. And some quiet.

This is why I like to forage. It takes me outside with my awareness intact so that I am ready to listen. I have much to learn. My friend C. comes to visit and we go out snowshoeing. We find tracks in the snow and try to read them. She teaches me to think about how the animal moves. She shows me the patterns: the hops of birds, feather-markings of turkey, the front-feet-back-feet patterns of the snowshoe hare. I love this new awareness. I am learning the language of my landscape.

The animal tracks are little journal entries. They tell the story of courage. The hare crosses an open spot, risking the chance that a hawk will spot her. She is vulnerable when she leaves tracks but the song of her heart tells her she cannot stand still. She must move.

Safety, like fear, kills us. It strips us of our vital energy, our feeling of being fully alive. It also could be killing our planet, slowly and steadily choking out the weeds while the approved genetically-engineered plants are tended and harvested in large flats of farms that are veritable strip mines.

And yet, I have made my choices too. I earn so little that I have been buying my flour and some bulk items at Walmart. I also shop locally but I appreciate the fact that the big box stores exist. My garden is not in full swing and I can't pay for a farm share, so I buy my bags of kale at the big store. I am no saint.

If that makes me vulnerable, then so be it. I give my truth to you. This is the song my heart sings and I am dancing to it.

YOGA FOR COURAGE

I have to admit that in spite of the way it all sounds in *Walking Away*, I don't always feel that courageous. That's why I practice yoga and look for ways to deepen my practice on a daily basis. Why yoga? I would have to say because the practice focuses a lot of attention on the heart which is the center of our courage.

Etymologically speaking, the English word *courage* gets its root from the Latin word for heart: *cor.* Much of the practice of yoga focuses its attention on expanding space in the area of the thorax, the heart, and the lungs, and strengthening the body's core.

Even if you've never taken a yoga class or caught one on tape to try in your living room, you can appreciate the simplicity of some of these poses. If you practice a lot of yoga, I'm sure your mind will scan all of the poses that are good for increasing courage.

The first pose is what I call superman/woman pose. You stand with your hands on your hips, elbows spread out side-to-side, and then lift up with the top area of your chest, drop your shoulders back, and keep your chin parallel to the floor. If ever you feel that someone is trying to overpower you or make you feel a little less than courageous, stand like this and you'll see how they back down a little. So simple. It also works to get someone's attention.

If you want to increase the impact on your own courageous demeanor, rotate your elbows back toward each other, thumbs on your lower spine (lumbar), and tilt your head back, gazing upward, expanding your heart center, and reaching with the chin toward the ceiling or sky.

The more you practice standing this way, the more it becomes habit. Dropping your shoulders and lifting up with your heart center is a subtle, yet powerful, method to feel and express personal power.

If you coordinate your breathing with this movement, you might notice that it enhances your ability to breathe more deeply and slowly. This increases the body's ability to absorb oxygen. More oxygen elevates the body's performance. More oxygen means more power in this equation.

Things don't have to be large and complex to be powerful. They just have to be heartfelt.

2. PARTS
October 8, 2013

Mike and I often say that love built our house. There were many times when we weren't sure that we would be able to do it but that's when we looked into each other's eyes, found the love there, and recharged our batteries. We know that we must both do our parts to stay positive if we are going to make this lifestyle work for us. We both have what I like to call the *can-do attitude* mixed with some discipline.

Our strategy for all problems is mathematical. We break things into parts, examine the parts, and then come up with steps. This often results in the twelve step process and it makes us laugh. To reach our goals, we remain vigilant, keep our priorities straight, and try to keep things as simple as possible. We both firmly believe that all things are possible if we just do our part to make things happen.

I often think about my great-grandmother, born in the Centennial of the United States (1876). She died just a few years before the Bicentennial. Family lore is that her mother sat on Lincoln's knee when she was a young girl.

Florence Brink was born in the Midwest on the brink of an explosion of technological innovation and a runaway cultural movement. She went from riding a horse and a covered carriage, to steam-powered trains and, finally, individual automobiles.

My great-grandmother had a *can-do* attitude and believed in love. She relied on its power exclusively. She practiced energy-healing, calling in the great love of what she called *Universal Mind* to pass through her to heal herself. She never once needed the care of a doctor, even when she severed her little finger with an icebox door. (They were really heavy back then.) According to family stories, she calmly found a length of ordinary tape and reattached her own little finger. In a matter of days, her finger was healed.

What really set Florence Brink apart, however, is that she fell in love with a foreign college student, studying business at the university in her home town. To say Jose was tall, dark and handsome would seem cliché, but it was true. A little too dark, maybe. He was from Southern Spain and his last name was Alarco (decidedly Moorish). Think *Othello*, and you might guess how anxious her parents felt about the union. After some hesitation, they finally conceded to their daughter's individuality and celebrated the wedding with love in their hearts.

In spite of their unusual beginnings, my great-grandparents created a loving family that still practices many of the same concepts of pushing the envelope that they did. I am guessing that I am not alone in my ancestry of forward-movers who followed the path of love and were busy creating new contexts. The United States got the handle, *melting pot*, for a reason.

As descendants of this group of trailblazers, we can't help but be a part of a larger context of Americans. This is a place where our ancestry can be so complex that we can only identify with the one that most fits our personalities or our phenotypes. But, like all parts of something, when you start to take us apart, you realize that we all share commonalities.

I met a young man from Tobago one time at a gathering who said, "It doesn't matter what shirt we were born wearing. Inside, we are all the same. Our hearts beat the same. Inside, our body parts are all the same color." I often think of that little slice of wisdom as a way to remember that our skins don't define us. Our skins are only the shirts we were born wearing. And skin, we all know, is a porous, living membrane that protects its wearer from disease. As we melt more and more into each other, we realize this wisdom. Ironically, this awareness gives us the courage to stand up straight and just be ourselves.

This understanding that each of us is an essential part of a whole binds us in a new context that has had a profound effect on the world as we know it.

Taking a thing apart, it seems, is the best way to understand the complexity of that thing's whole. Much like untangling a mess of rope, all critical thinkers know, taking things apart and taking things in steps is the way to solve problems.

As a society, we are able to move forward if our coming together is made up of individuals who are true to themselves. This creates a healthy cycle that can move forward. Like each spoke of a wheel, we must each stand proud if we want to be able to drive that wheel down the rocky road of a nation's issues. To clarify, each part of our nation must be healthy. Its survival depends entirely on each of us doing our parts to make that happen.

If we find ourselves looking too hard at a whole problem, it is almost impossible to solve that problem.

Building a house is a perfect example of using that strategy. It grows in layers. Some layers, like a roof or windows, are a little more important than others.

Recently, I listened in on a conversation about children and how our society limits their ability to release natural aggression. The participants in the discussion were members of the Maine Primitive Skills School community and they were lamenting that more and more tweens are practicing self-mutilation as a result of pent-up aggressions.

The new buzzword in schools is "bullying" and we try to teach our kids to *just say no* to it. Admirable, for sure, but it seems, once again, that what we resist, will persist.

What solutions do my "primitive" friends propose? Some say, allow kids to run through the forest with pocket knives again. Translation: bring back playing outside. It was in the old *sandlot* that hierarchies were created and dismantled. This is where an individual developed personal power and learned how to defend him or herself in a world where these skills are sorely needed. It also was a place where circles were formed, alliances made, and family ties strengthened. In short, when children were unsupervised, they found themselves in a place where the spokes of a wheel can be forged and tempered.

It is possible you are thinking about William Golding's, *Lord of the Flies,* since it is mandatory ninth-grade reading in most schools. The characters in the story find themselves on a deserted island without adults and they create a cruel, chaotic world at war with itself. (According to biographical accounts, Golding himself was an odd, frustrated youth who reported he enjoyed bullying others.)

Popular culture is not healthy for our young. Commercialism is not at fault here. The video companies are only responding to the needs of our children, the need to safely act out their natural aggression. But, in many cases, this virtual world of constant hostility isn't helping them move forward. A virtual experience just isn't the same as the real thing.

⊗How often do we find ourselves doing all of the household chores while our kids are in their rooms bonding with technology? Probably more than we would like to admit. Maybe the answer is to require them to do their part. When Mike and I were kids we were required to do chores. We often laugh about how our generation did the chores when we were kids, did them for our kids, and then do them for our parents. We don't lament the first and third in that list but the middle one is cause for concern. Doing chores taught us that we were valuable members of a family. Our parents needed us and that is a good thing. The scenario is a little unnatural when thirty-somethings need their parents to survive. The kids need to start doing their parts if we want the family picture to be complete.

Perhaps a little more work and a little more recess might help. Let's face it, recess is important for the adults too. A little recess from TV, phone, or computer time might be good for everyone. A dinner plate might replace the paper plate and require kids to do some dishes. More work and more unstructured play time might not be the full solution but it might be a good place to start.

Sometimes taking things apart reveals different problems. Kids fight a lot when they are free to play. We might have to be willing to make things worse if we want to ultimately make things better. Dishes might fill the sink for some days. Cabinets might contain greasy plates. Kids might fight over whose turn it is. Subtle changes might require a little tough love.

Some of us are concerned that our children are spending more time gazing at a screen than in the eyes of someone who loves them. Maybe that is because the adults in their lives are gazing at screens too. If we approach our most troubling problems in steps, maybe the first step could be to prioritize our energies and to apply some self-discipline. It might mean a little more reaching out than shutting out. Maybe it's time for my great-grandmother's *can-do attitude* and asking everyone, in spite of age, background, personality, or ability to do their parts. It might require a little more love, even if it's the tough kind. Our future depends on it.

MECHANICAL HEALING

Mike has always understood mechanics. His father was known to repair car engines inside the house in the winter. Mike has done the same thing. I could look at it as annoying but I tend to think anybody who can fix things the way he does is marvelous. I guess that's why we get along. Life with him is messy yet fascinating.

For one thing, we drive old cars because those are the ones Mike understands. It is a rare occasion when we have to take our car in to a mechanic. And, well, you'll hear about that in a later chapter.

Living in a small town, far from concentrated populations, requires a car or two. Driving down dirt roads treated with calcium chloride and roads that get torn up from excessive ice and rain are a sure recipe for trouble when it comes to mechanical upkeep. You could drive a big truck but life requires some travel time and you have to factor the cost of fuel in the equation.

It's a balancing act and you could say, "Gee whiz, why don't you just get one good car?" and we would say, "Well, newer cars break down too." The only difference is they also have so many computerized features that a common mechanic can't fix them so you end up having to spend so much money and worse, *time,* as you do your best to save up enough money to pay for them to be *diagnosed.*

For Mike, understanding how our cars work is key. He is not afraid to get under the car, in the engine, or stick his upper body out of the door while the car is travelling down the road to get a good look. He is also not afraid to make the situation worse by taking everything apart. Google helps. Being able to imagine how to accomplish something with no tools is helpful.

For instance, Sherman the Tank had a grinding noise in the rear axle. Mike was pretty sure it was the differential oil. When he googled how to replace the oil, the person who posted said, "Have a set of wrenches and paper towels ready. The wrenches are to remove the plug but they are so tight that you'll need the paper towels to wipe the blood off of your knuckles."

Mike decided that he would avoid the knuckle bleed and try attaching a come-along to the wrench, attaching the other end to the chassis of the car. I can always tell when his ingenuity works (which honestly, is most of the time) because he comes out smiling and dancing the high-five dance. But then he had to get the oil into the differential without removing most of the chassis. He used a tube feed with a funnel and attached that to the back door latch to hold it in place. It worked.

This may not seem like much, but to us it was a $300-$400 savings and since he did it on a Sunday, he was able to drive it to work on Monday. Because of Mike's willingness to chance taking things apart and his creative approaches, we manage to keep moving.

3. EDGES
April 26, 2014

A lot of people said that building a house together is the worst thing for a marriage. We say it has been the best thing. That doesn't mean it has been the easiest thing.

When Mike and I met about twelve years ago, he wanted to get married. I was nervous, but after some time, I trusted my parents' and family's opinions and most of all, my own heart. My heart told me that I would be okay, that here was love.

Our budget for the wedding was limited since we were putting all of our resources into providing a clean safe place for the kids. Starting over has its costs. Budgeting for my wedding dress was low on the list; I had about $200 to work with. But the minute I saw it, I knew that there had been divine intervention at foot. It may seem a little trite to anyone who hasn't had to do it, but choosing a wedding dress is nothing less than a spiritual experience, at least in my case. I guess you could also say that everything is a spiritual experience in my case.

I had been concerned that it was all happening way too soon. My first marriage had been a traumatic experience and I had met Mike within months after the break-up. *It was a rebound,* I heard my friends say; *be careful,* I had to tell myself. *This is too good to be true,* I worried. Nevertheless, it was true. And though fear could have easily paralyzed me and kept me from allowing the rhythm of life to take me forward, I fell in love.

In the story-telling of our lives, we are not much different than most modern couples. We came together, two wounded warriors, finding in each other a little bit of restoration. A broken heart seems to work better, as flawed as it is. It takes nothing for granted. It gives completely and honestly, knowing that it can heal and always will. Usually. Yet, as all healers know, it takes some time and patience.

There are times when, tired and stretched thin, our old wounds open. Building a house will push your limits, for sure. This is when our hearts leak energy and we lose the will to keep things up. This is the tough part about being human. We can't avoid pushing our limits.

All relationships have their raw edges. Like cogs in the gears of life, our edges are what propel us forward, forcing us to take a good hard look at ourselves and decide it is time to grow. We don't like the way our edges sometimes rip into the fabric of our peace but we can't help it. We are just built that way.

Nothing is entirely smooth when you get close enough to really see. The surface of the earth is ragged and coarse but looks like a smooth bubble from the surface of the moon. Love is the spaceship that lands on another person's surface and lets us see the reality that even the silken texture of desert sand is made up of abrasive little rocks. We get that close.

Recently, Mike and I experienced a breakdown in our relationship. I like to think of it more as a *breakthrough*. This is when truth, hard cold truth, is like gunpowder in our guts. We try desperately to keep it under wraps, locked-up tight from any moisture. Then Kaboom!! There it goes, all the truth we have been storing up flies out of us in all directions. It could have been better.

Allowing truth to burst through isn't always easy or safe but it will keep us from leading an empty existence. It's not always the stuff that we want to look at but it is the most powerful thing we own. Giving ourselves the license to be honest with each other is the finest gift we can give to ourselves and to those whom we love. But it does a number on our trust. I have found that it is best to keep truth on the backburner. That way it keeps me warm rather than explosive.

It is all too easy to get defensive with each other. Being defensive only serves to force our partners to keep their truths bottled up because they don't want to get into a skirmish with us. They let things go that bother them because they can't talk about it with us. Bottled up truths ferment and are a recipe for disaster.

So what do you do when your truth does blow up? What happens when something that has been kept in and choked down finally finds its way to the surface and you can no longer keep it to yourself? There's a lot of scrambling around, trying to stuff it all back in, but it's got a force too great to be controlled and can leave a wake of broken emotions and nerves with raw edges.

All of us suffer in some way; it might be why we are here. For some of us, the suffering starts when we are very young. We deal with the constant struggle of feeling unwanted. We harbor deep tissue memories of rejection and exclusion and these memories linger in our psyches like a child in a dirt pile, kicking up dust and clouding out sunshine.

Rejection can then be compounded by a marriage that ends in betrayal. It can continue with every relationship thereafter.

You might meet people who have experienced these things and can't see through the cloud. Or they might be the ones who bring sunshine to everyone else. But then these people will have their days, when alone in their vehicles they will cry uncontrollably. They are the ones who use an advanced sense of humor to get them through their own lives of internal combat. But doing so has a price. Perhaps they keep their truth in too small a pot on that backburner. It is bound to boil over sometimes.

As for me, I had a good, loving childhood but experienced a painful first marriage of acute duplicity. I too have a pot of truth on the backburner but its content scalds. I must place my truth in small cups and wait a little before I can sip at it. It is best when I give it the time.

Perhaps that's what is needed to keep our truths from overheating. Maybe we need to spend a little time with our truths, stirring it, adding water, and other ingredients. Maybe it's good to share our truths in circles of love. When we share our truths, we can create a stone soup. Whatever we make together might not be appetizing but it could keep us from dying inside.

Living next to the river has its advantages. Why not allow some of that gunpowder to get damp? It is one way to destabilize it. Maybe those people's tears in their vehicles are exactly what is required for them to deal with explosive truths. But maybe doing so only shores up their defenses and they end up alone, cringing behind fortress walls. Holding tight to a defensive position is no way to win an internal war.

Maybe sharing our tears will help to expose our gunpowder truths, destabilize our ammo a little and help us realize that our defensive position stems from the fear that love will abandon us someday for something better. The truth is that people abandon us, not love. The message love wants us to hear is that we are always free to go if a situation damages our ability to love ourselves. Love is loyal and will return to us again and again if we let it.

Often, our truth boils down to a lack of communication. Moving forward means to try very hard to communicate; to look in the direction of the other person and say, "I'm sorry." As feeble as it sounds, it's an opening. It might take a few days for the hurt to untangle its grip on our hearts, but we trust that it will. It is the willingness to shift a perspective, wait for the right moment to speak our truths, and try to change ourselves (since we can't change anyone else).

So, when I look into Mike's eyes and I see withdrawal after the cogs of our gears are out of alignment and my little tea cups of truth have scalded my tongue, I trust that underneath the lizard eye of cold protection is his deep brown eye of unconditional love. His gaze is a little stubborn and only will give when it is ready, but I trust that it will eventually be ready. We know we must get our gears back in sync so we can move forward again. We have a job to do and our lives depend on it.

The ability to move forward is uniquely pertinent when it comes to building a house off the grid. We have to be able to work together or we will likely suffer disaster. Trusting in each other and moving forward are essential components of our lifestyle. We have to be able to survive the gritty, raw edges of life, do our best to smooth them out, and concentrate on the big picture where it all looks silky.

The day we all drew together to participate in our wedding, we did so under the canopy of trees. With the guidance of a minister of faith, we made promises to each other, to the Creative Power of attraction, and to our loved ones. We did so in the embrace of nature and under the warm light of the sun. We needed no human structure to shelter our faith. Our promise was, that in spite of the inevitable turbulence we would experience together, we would face each other and look inward, not away.

The day I walked down the crunchy, leaf-strewn isle with my father by my side, and stood with my daughters, my brother, my mother, and my cousins, I looked into Mike's eyes to seal in my trust. We all trusted him that day. We all knew that you can't always take for granted that you can trust the other person in a relationship but we were all willing to try again.

What I have learned is that my trust in myself is most important. I had trusted that in the great Love of the Universe, the right partner would come to me. When it happened, I had to trust in my heart that I would know it was right. I had to trust in this person that he would respect my kids. I had to trust in my kids that they would try their best to respect themselves and him while they grew.

I had to trust in myself that it if it didn't work out, I would listen to my heart and survive the fallout. And I had to trust that he would be able to also trust in all of these things.

So what moves us from *breakdown* to *breakthrough*? It is remembering that what binds us together is the trust. What we knew on that day was to keep looking toward each other until we can see eye-to-eye. It is remembering that in the beginning, when we all gathered around to witness the promises, we were all trusting in each other that this union of two people's lives and two families would be a good thing. It is remembering that, though exposing our truths can shake things up sometimes, ultimately, it is all worth it.

There are always those who cry at weddings and they're not sure why. I am one of them. Sure the bride looks radiant and the room is filled with hopeful exuberance, but I think it is more than that. A wedding is symbolic of the fact that every day we wake up, we trust that, in spite of our imperfections and life's trials, we will be okay, that love will not desert us.

Weddings are the ultimate in dancing on life's edge of trust. They remind us of the importance of love, family unity, and being able to take long looks into the eyes of those we are committed to. Living in love requires that both parties are able to search out the eyes of trust again and again, even when the mind builds its fortresses. Without these treaties of trust, we simply cannot love. Some could argue that we could not live either.

On our wedding day, I made my promises in the perfect dress because, though the truth was I didn't have nearly enough money to buy a suitable wedding dress, I had trusted that I would find it. My dress found me on the sales rack of an ordinary department store. The dress spoke to me and said, "Yes, this is the symbol you will wear." It was composed of uneven strips of natural, undyed silk with frayed edges and I felt brilliant in it. It was my private symbol of knowing that in order to truly live, you have to allow love to return to you, be able to handle the truth, remember to trust, and to see the beauty in life's raw edges.

STINGING NETTLES

Nettles are a lot like relationships. They aren't always easy to hold on to but are really worth the effort. Once you consider the health benefits of adding stinging nettle to your diet, you will want to encourage it to grow in your weed beds (the only kind I presently own!).

A little research on this plant will reveal to you why so many people consider it their favorite plant. I know people who make beers from it, they love it so much. I dehydrate mine to use it in winter soups and stews. I have also added it to my tea blends. Either way, it will add important vitamins, minerals, and phytochemicals to your diet.

Common stinging nettles are used for food and medicine. In fact, there are so many health benefits and medicinal qualities to nettles that it is a wonder we don't see them in grocery stores in little plastic containers next to spinach. It is wonderful for iron deficiency, trouble in the urinary tract, issues with the prostate, skin and hair ailments (including eczema), and is good for pregnant women because it helps stem internal bleeding.

The nutritional value of nettles include significant source of iron, potassium, calcium, and silica. They also are a significant source of vitamin A, B-Complex, vitamin C, and vitamin K. The combination of these vitamins help the body absorb the iron so nettle tea has been used for centuries as a tonic for anemia.

Use gloves and long sleeves when harvesting stinging nettle. The little hairs along the stems can be caustic but the intense burning usually only lasts a half an hour. Once you dry the plant or cook it, the plant no longer stings so preparation is easy. Nettle leaves will dry out in the sun in a few hours.

4. ALCHEMY
May 17, 2014

Mike and I are constantly engaged in transmutations of the mind. Changing the heart and the mind are how we grow. Because our plow truck burned last winter, we were forced to trudge through thick snow the half mile from the road to our house. That's not so bad until you add that we were routinely loaded down with groceries, laundry, and propane tanks. But we were truly happy because it forced us to be outside a little more at night and we were able to witness shooting stars. By looking up instead of down, we changed our reality. Changing our perspectives changes our minds. Instead of focusing on our cold feet, we were able to see the beauty of the night sky. Out here, it is a spectacle worth seeing.

We both understand the power of creativity and take it seriously. It is how we have been able to build our house together. The way I see it, there is gold in attuning the ability to constantly choose to see the stars, trusting that they are there, even on cloudy nights. Keeping the dream alive is all about attitude.

The way I have heard it is alchemists were the early scientists. We're talking about 2,000 years before Christ. They called themselves *Hermetics*, after Hermes Trismegistus, the Greek messenger God, the only being able to traverse into all three worlds: Olympus, Earth, and Hades. These early knowledge-seekers eventually were from a variety of religious and cultural backgrounds. They would gather together to understand the nature of all things in this world and beyond. Intent on understanding the motives and methods of the Great Creator, they ultimately argued over dogma, since, by nature, that knowledge is beyond human understanding. As a result, they all agreed that in their discussions, they would omit any reference whatsoever to the Divine Architect. Coming from a diversity of cultures and faiths, it was the only way they could move on to try and understand what was within their reach. Alchemists then became scientists.

Naturally, the people of their day were more interested in the transmutation of metals (a secret method of creating gold!) than in the spiritual alchemy. There's no profit to be made in the purification of souls so if an alchemist wanted any kind of funding, he had to work his metals. This eventually led to a transmutation of the art itself and to its eventual discredit since it was only half of its original self.

Some might argue that a science that does not accept a higher power is limited. It will be focused solely on the matter we can see and hold. It is incapable of seeing the big picture. It proceeds, sometimes, with methods that are contrary to nature and goodness. Some might say it has led humans to play God with life.

What is interesting to me is how today's science is focusing more than ever on the big picture. And the little one too. Check out the research being done on micro-biomes and it will blow your mind. If the Buddhists are right and we are all one, then quantum physicists and micro-biologists have the science to prove it. Whatever you want to call it, science is looking for this higher power and is discovering its traces.

How does this relate to a common person just wanting to do the right thing while alive? The way I see it is, since we are all connected, it's important to do our part. If we intend to be upbeat and part of something upbeat, we must first work on ourselves. Like a scientist's crucible, it is imperative that our hearts be clean of unwanted substances that could influence the outcome of our efforts. When we recognize the importance of self-reflection and study ways to keep ourselves in good working order, physically, mentally, and spiritually, the outcome should be okay.

We also must recognize human nature. Seeing things for what they are instead of what we would like them to be helps us maintain a keen, objective, and neutral attitude. Happiness depends, for the most part, on remaining untainted by any assumptions about life. All ego or need to be right serve only to inhibit understanding of the true nature of things. The more we understand, the less likely we are to take things personally.

The way Mike and I see it is, you may as well have fun while you're here. Life is always going to present its challenges. Problems give us an opportunity to be creative. Our problems are our solutions. We also see the force of creativity as divine and when we create, we get to feel how we are a part of the bigger picture.

Nothing, I have found, blocks creativity more than self-absorption and self-judgement. Preconceived notions almost never are accurate and can block us from seeing the real solution. Nothing clears the way for solutions to a problem better than focusing on the big picture and having a good laugh and a little fun. Ultimately, the goal is to find a graceful solution to whatever the challenge *du jour* is.

I have come to think that all of life is a science of discovery. We imperfectly waddle our way through its winding paths and all arrive home, worn and in need of rest. But, if we stop to look around us during the journey, we discover that there are things to restore us along the way; we just have to notice. I suppose that is what alchemists do. They notice that life is full of beauty. There are stars out there when we take the time to look. When our lives are too full of artificial light, we don't always notice.

Sitting next to the river, I observe the way that the ferns unfurl themselves this time of year; I am reminded of my own life's unfurling. Picking dandelions, I think about how bright-faced I can be when I choose to reflect the light of nature's beauty. It is always there for the taking but it requires a certain innocence.

I think dandelions are the ultimate alchemists, transmuting an anemic, gravelly soil into a golden source of power. Her root is more valuable than any other for healing the human body.

Foragers are alchemists, seeking the secrets of the field and forest, in full appreciation of nature's bounty. They seek graceful solutions to thriving and healing. Foraging takes clarity, patience, and a lot of study. It takes reverent intentions, gratitude, and a willingness to understand divine creativity.

In some ways, it is the return to the Garden from which we expelled ourselves. Through humility and integrity, nature assures us, we are always welcome back. We can, once again, find our peaceful place with the Creator's plan if we so choose.

We possess the power to choose heaven over hell at any time. It happens one step at a time, one thought at a time.

Seeing things from a different perspective, we cease the chemical war on our brothers and sisters and we begin to return to the Garden nature has planted for us.

We accept the wilderness in ourselves too. Like our little rectangular plots of perfectly manicured lawns and flower beds all buttoned up in neat little rows, our minds are groomed and squared off so that we fit in small spaces together. No weeds can grow here. Our neighbors will complain. Weeds, after all, are highly contagious. We must administer the proper chemicals to control them.

Perhaps what we truly need is a little space to stretch and reach in organic ways. Perhaps what our children need is to dig in the dirt, hug a tree, and eat a dandelion raw, just like that, without wondering if it is coated with weed-killer or has absorbed lead. Maybe we need to approach our children as an alchemists would, disciplining ourselves as the crucibles, seeking to understand human nature, seeing the bigger picture, and ultimately waiting for the graceful solution to reveal itself to us.

Alchemists know the influence of negative thought patterns such as doubt and fear, seeing them clearly as implements of the dark forces. If given to entertaining these emotions, alchemists know they will manifest fears and doubts.

When looking out over our carefully planted green carpet interrupted by spots of yellow, do we see a nuisance or do we see gold? Sustainable is not just a new buzzword; it is an idea that humans need to revisit. It is the transmutation of human thought and action. It is taking the accepted idea of scarcity and melting it in the crucible of one's own being, allowing abundance. It is nothing less than the transmutation of human awareness.

GOLDENROD TEA

According to history, when the early American Colonists threw bundles of tea overboard during the Boston Tea Party, they might not have been ready for the full consequences of their exuberance. For one thing, if you really want to get a Brit *t'd-off*, mess with his tea. For another thing, it never did get rid of high and unfair taxes.

No one knows if the colonists were also ready for a life without tea, at least the caffeinated kind you get from China. What we do know is that they learned from the Native Americans and drank goldenrod tea as a substitute. They did so until things could get settled and they could find a way to grow their own tea.

Using the flower of this prolific plant produces an aromatic, golden tea that is as healthy as it is pretty.

Anyone can drink it but it is particularly good for folks who suffer from kidney problems. The tea from goldenrod flowers can help break up kidney stones while it rinses out the kidneys. It is beneficial for anyone who is prone to urinary tract infections, as well.

As with any herbal tea, consult a doctor if you are taking any medications. You might have to also avoid it if it messes with your allergies. If you're all clear, you just dry out a few good handfuls of the flowers and then pinch off a little for your teapot.

Heat the water first, then add the tea (try not to boil your teas). Let it steep for six minutes, strain, and pour.

5. WHAT RUSH
June 10, 2014

When I think about my girls, (which, by the way, is all of the time), I think about needing to do, be, or get somewhere sometime soon. It is hard to shift from all of the rushing that most of family life and all of its schedules and immediacies required to a relaxed and neutral state, but it happens. In my case it has taken a little time. I keep having to remind myself that it's okay if I can't make the four-and-a-half hour drive to see them because I now have my own schedule and it doesn't easily mesh with theirs. Besides, I don't like to leave Hermes (my dog) home alone all day.

You can't rush the river. It must run its own course. Rain will happen. Ice flows in the spring will strip the bark off the trees and you might believe that the trees could never survive such a trauma. But they do. You think it will ruin the photogenic nature of the river. The river is more beautiful as a result.

Since most scenery in these parts is absent of human influence, it's not uncommon to see people taking pictures on the side of the road. You think, by their concentration, they've spotted a moose. Sometimes, all they want, however, is to capture the miracle of the reflection of a line of bark-stripped trees leaning impossibly over a scalped river bank. The ice flow has caused massive destruction. It is stunningly beautiful.

Let's face it, we all have compromised bark, but we survive life's scrapings. And it does make us more beautiful. It's the trees that are a little twisted or different that are always more interesting and sometimes most valuable to us, growing burls and lovely birds-eye grains, and golden flashes.

The scraped trees are the ones that grow the best mushrooms. One of them is the black fungus and shelf mushrooms that form as scabs on the damaged bark of white and yellow birch trees. Shelf mushrooms are proving to be some of nature's most beneficial medicines for man.

Worrying about my family seems to be a theme I return to again and again and I realize that it is time to move on but I have not been able to rush it. Though for my girls and me, ours is a story with its pain, it is not unique. It is not the story that makes the difference, it is the beauty that remains after the scraping that matters to anyone. It is a testament to others to say, *see, there is, eventually, an outcome. Just hold on; it may not be pretty now but it will be some day.* That day, you will look back. You may be writing a book that you're not sure anyone will read, and you will say, *yes, my reflection in the river of life is beautiful. Take a picture because this is proof that you too will survive. And your scars may be exactly what you need to help others with their bruises and deeper wounds.*

In this remote life by the river, the worst danger is the impulse to rush. Nature takes her time. If there's one thing I have learned out here, it is that it is best to pay attention to her temperament. Any false step could mean a path of trouble we need not travel. Any hiker who has ever gotten lost will tell you that.

Simple things like trying to move the small rota-tiller while carrying a load of other things, can mess you up.

"I'll get that later," Mike told me while we were working in the garden. I know better, I think, *no he won't. The tiller will sit out in the rain and then he'll have to fix it next time he needs it.* So, I proceed to try and get it with my left hand, dragging it across the large roll of PVC sheeting we saved for greenhouse construction. It is expensive stuff and we have carefully stored it for a while. If you guessed that the tiller blade cut right through several layers of the sheeting, you'd be almost right; it cut through probably more than that. (Sad face here.)

Mike was calm. "So, I guess you see why it's better not to rush into things and try to do it all yourself."

Yes, I say. *Yes. It is always better to be deliberate in my thoughts and actions. And, to accept that I don't have to do it all myself. This is true.* I don't have to feel like I am responsible for the outcome of everything that goes on in my life. This is a hard concept for me to accept. Perhaps I would have less anxiety about it all if I had been able to be more of a fatalist in this existentialist, self-help, self-betterment, low-cholesterol, time management, buns of steel, race-to-the-top kind of society in which I find myself.

Rushing, I think, is a personal responsibility thing. Taking responsibility for what happens to us and who we are requires some effort and *we'd better just get out there and get it done or we're going to fall apart. Talking never got the soup cooked. Actions speak louder than words.* You are what you eat. You know.

A young friend asks my philosophical opinion, "If you don't care so much, is it really a problem?"

I don't know.

Perhaps what we need is to just slow the river that flows through us. Perhaps we need to create the mirrored pool of calm and look into it and say, *yes, it is beautiful. It is raw and peeled, and impossible, but it is beautiful. Take a picture people, because this is life. And it is beautiful. It is an open laugh caught on film that makes your eyes look really small, your nose huge, and you can see all of those fillings in your teeth. It is you. And you've survived. And you're laughing.*

Acceptance and calm requires no rush to quickly delete it or cover it up and say, *I'm not photogenic.* Acceptance and calm reminds us that there is no need to fear the river of life. It will rage and tear at us some days and will be calm and peaceful other days. Life will have its seasons and we may as well just dig our roots in deeply and hang on to its shores to weather it all. And one of these days, an ice flow might come along and we'll be ripped right out by the roots and will float downstream. But if we're lucky, some of our seeds will have sprouted and the space our absence creates will provide good soil for new growth.

I just hope those little seedlings learn how to laugh until their faces crack in half and don't rush around trying to make it all seem perfect. I hope they realize there's no need to delete the pictures of their lives, seeking the perfect image. I hope they don't blame me for planting them right on the river's edge. I'm sorry, it's where I was planted too. It's a risky place to try and grow, I know but, *it is all so beautiful.*

AUTUMN OLIVE JAM

I always make sure I have enough of this jam on hand for my girls because they both love it. They also love the Autumn Olive fruit leather (see Chapter 9 for tips on making fruit leathers). Having these two things stocked up when they come to visit makes them very happy they took the time and chanced the drive.

I feel the need to include this recipe because there are a few recipes out there for A-O jam that don't set up right so I figured I would save you some *trial and error* time. If you happen to find autumn olive berries growing near you, it's worth it to try this jam, even if you HATE jam. You'll love this one. Trust me.

*Sterilize your jelly jars by boiling them in your canner.

*Take 8 cups of whole berries. (No need to remove the little stems - it's a waste of time. Do take the leaves out, though.)

*Add 1 cup water. Simmer whole berries for 20 minutes.

*Use a hand-powered food mill to mash and remove seeds. You can use a colander but it takes a lot of time and you'll need to start with 9 cups of whole berries, if you do. This should make 5 cups of mash.

*Add 3 cups sugar

*Mix ½ cup sugar with **NO-sugar sure jell**

Bring to a rolling boil, add sure jell mixture. Boil one minute. Carefully pour into your sterilized jars, place the caps on and hand-tighten the rings. Boil in your large water canner (or a big pot with a layer of canning rings on the bottom to make a rack) with the lid on for 20 minutes. Turn the heat off and let sit for five minutes before removing the jars. According to my notes, it makes 9 jelly jars.

According to my experience, **you must use the no-sugar pectin.** Otherwise, just use your "jam" as a tasty sauce or throw it in your dehydrator for fruit leather. It just won't set up if you use regular or homemade pectin.

Autumn Olive fruit leather is really good, so don't throw away any of your jam.

6. NO JOB TOO
June 12, 2014

Last time I wrote about not having a job, I wrote about spontaneously foraging with our friends Heather and Glenn. I may have been a little smug about it because I indeed did have a job. I was BUILDING A HOUSE. There's no job more direct and satisfying than that. Now that we are living in the house (unfinished, of course), house-building is just an endless to-do list of details that can pile up and overwhelm. Add to that the clutter of moving from a large house with lots of storage to a small house with none yet, and you get the idea of what that list looks like. You might also get an idea of what the basement and, *horrors...*, the guest bedroom looks like. So, what does a responsible adult do under these circumstances? She runs away as fast as she can to get busy doing something else!

That's not the only reason I applied for a high school English position at the nearby academy. In spite of my reluctance, one of Mike's customers convinced me to apply for it, claiming that I would be a perfect fit. I guess my conversation on the job was better than my tiling abilities. But, the primary reason I applied for the job was because I truly like to teach.

Both Mike and I constantly pray that we will be directed by the higher forces to be of most use wherever we find ourselves. We know, because of everything we have been through, that those who dedicate their lives to service live happier lives. Before you think we are poster children for Kiwanis, just accept the fact that we are both very pragmatic and loving people. That should settle it.

So when I didn't get the English position at the academy, I wondered what was wrong with me. Did I not have enough talent to fill the job description? I went around for a few days mulling that over and decided that I just wasn't good enough for the job. Even though I may have thought that it is a shame that someone who loves teaching and literature so completely would not be given a chance to share it with the starving minds of today's youth, the bare truth was that the administration at the school did not see it that way. Perhaps, I believed myself to be more important than I really am. Always a possibility.

As usual, Mike's calm and supportive nature kicked in and he reminded me that I *always* focus on the negative of every situation. So true, what the heck is wrong with me anyway? *Why am I so negative?*

This is when I thought, *this has to be a chapter.* I can work these things out on paper as I have always done and the unsuspecting reader won't care that I'm so negative. And, by the way, so darned poor that I can't even afford to get my hair cut in town; my husband has to do it for me! *Maybe that's why I didn't get the job.* This is when I think, *yes, time to stop being so negative about it.* My hair was just fine during the interview and no one cares what your hair looks like anyway. What mattered during my interview is that I was completely myself and I know my truth is the most powerful thing I own. So, if my truth doesn't fit their job description, then I don't belong in that position anyway.

The truth is, when Mike and I look for direction, we really mean it. Sometimes (I'm not saying every time), the Universe has other plans for us. It might mean a spell of really tight budgeting, of making more couch-cushion dinners, of home-made haircuts, and other creative solutions, but it also means having to lean in really close and listen really hard to know what the right plan is. Because it's hard to see right at that moment. Let's face it, when you don't get what you want, especially if you worked really hard to get it, what you really get is faith.

For a moment, you might lose faith in yourself, but it comes back in little bits, because you have to have faith in yourself, or your partner will tell you to stop being so negative. And when you stop to think about it, having a positive attitude is an obligation to our partners. Otherwise, the whole structure of friendship tumbles and no amount of therapy will keep it up until both parties decide to think positively again. Try as we might, it's not the amount of money we bring in that makes the structure strong. It's our positive attitudes that do it.

So when I scan back on the little extra-money fantasies I had of being able to help the girls, save some money, finish the house, and do some travelling, I have to accept the fact that our dreams and our destinies are separate. A truly integrated human being listens closely to the divine whisper and unites these two parts of himself. Perhaps what I should pray for is assistance with uniting my dream with my destiny.

And then it occurs to me that sitting in front of a keyboard (it was my grandfather's typewriter when I was just a tot), has been my only true dream. Teaching literature fed that dream but it wasn't my destiny or I would still be doing it. Perhaps what I worked so hard to achieve by having that respectable job was stability. Perhaps it was the very same stability that was keeping my dream from ever catching up with my destiny. Being comfortable was an unstable place for my destiny. Perhaps what my destiny needs from me is to let go of the comfort and sink into the simplicity of owning my days.

Life without a job means that I am in charge of my days. If it is a rainy day and I would rather not address the cluttered back bedroom or organize the basement as I had planned, so be it. I have an important job to do. I must record all of the things we have experienced and all of the ways we have met our needs and how Mike and I have made life better for ourselves. Simply, we are learning to rely more on nature and ourselves, and must share what we have learned with others.

I ask myself, *so why did I ever jump off the platform of simplicity and try so hard to get back to my old respectable profession?* I think of Thoreau's advice: "Never look back unless that's where you want to go." Why I ever thought that it would be a good idea to get back in the ring, obviously not a spring chicken, and compete with candidates in their twenties, is something to consider. Besides being able to remember people's names better, kids relate more easily to younger teachers. It is natural.

Add up my love of teaching literature, that almost everyone I talked to encouraged me in some way to get back into teaching, and that we all know how important it is to have money and you end up with all the pressure I needed to suspend my destiny for a while as I reverted back to my old teacher ways (Yikes, did I just write that?).

I found myself rescuing wool blazers out of my give-away bag. I began to wear only the earrings with an equal partner instead of mixing them up so I can wear the earrings that I lost one OF. I began thinking, *I must be careful not to end a sentence with a preposition; everyone will notice.*

I began to get choked up in front of my keyboard. Words were not flowing for me as they had been. Careful grammar is the enemy of good writing. I am sure of it. In fact, it's what I would tell my writers in school. Write. Then edit. Use the rules of grammar to make or break your meaning. Time to return to teaching myself.

So, what must I get done today? I must find a way to make ends meet again. I think of the jobs my grandmother did as the wife of a writer and I think about Mike's assertion that whatever was useful to our grandparents is something we might consider today. And I think that it is time to revisit my function of finding ways to spend less money rather than ways of making more.

So, I put on my rubber boots and headed outside with Hermes. He gets ecstatic when he sees me in my boots because he knows we are about to forage. I pack up my foraging bag and add the mushroom knife and brush Mike gave me since it's about that time. I decide to collect some wildflowers for our dinner salad, hoping I'll find sweet plantain leaves in our gravelly yard. I noticed that two seasons after we excavated for the foundation of the house, we are starting to see yarrow, red clover, dandelion, sheep's quarters, and mountain cress growing cheerfully in the sandy, rocky soil. This makes me happy.

When John, the excavator, came back with some commercial grass seeds to spread, we told him not to bother; we like weeds. He laughed when we asked if he ever tried milkweed and he had replied that he'd never be so unfortunate.

When his work was complete and we paid him with an envelope of bills and two dozen oatmeal-raisin cookies, I told him that we'd share some of our harvest with him next fall but we'd keep the weeds to ourselves. Let's just say that we found another friend.

So, I think back to my writing, and I think, yes, it is full of weeds and odd things that we haven't identified yet and it's a bit scraggly and there may not be too many who are willing to try to read it. But, as I told our computer tech friend while envying his weedy garden, "You've got some great salad greens going there! Probably more nutritious than the ones you planted!"

He responded with genuine interest and wants to take a "weed walk" with me some day. I think, *Okay, maybe people will want to read about the wonders of weeds and weeding out unnecessary thoughts, and conditioning.* Maybe the world is ready for a little untamed prose too.

I think about our friend, Heather, who is the ultimate weed walker and how I would love to see her today for some mushrooming but I know she's not available because, well, she's got a job right now.

MILKWEED SOUP

If you pressure-can some chopped milkweed pods in the late summer, you can use them to make a lovely creamed soup in the winter. With a good crusty loaf of bread and a healthy slab of butter, this makes a remarkable dinner in the winter.

One of the best things about preserving summer food, especially food you foraged yourself, is that it reminds you of the beauty and abundance of summer when you might be a little closed in by the scarcity of winter. The greens you get in grocery stores this time of year are usually expensive and wilted. Add that to the narrowing of the light and dinners can be a recipe for melancholy. It helps to be creative about your greenery in the winter.

That's why I can milkweed. It makes a tasty creamed soup if you add some sautéed onions, a half cup of good milk, a little butter, salt, pepper, and Provence seasoning to a blender. It is so simple and easy.

Collect your green pods when they are small enough to contain white seeds and silky white fluff inside them. They are best if they are no larger than your thumb (about 2") but are useful as long as they contain white the silk. As soon as the seeds turn brown, they cannot be used. Chop the pods into halves or thirds. Boil them for at least three minutes. Change out the water and boil again for three minutes. This will remove any latex that the pods contain.

To pressure can, sterilize the jars by boiling them in clean water for a few minutes. Fill quart jars with your cooked milkweed pods, leaving a ½ inch headspace. Add clean boiled water and a half a teaspoon of salt for every quart jar. Dry the jar edges and place the lids on, hand-tightening the rings. Don't overly tighten the rings since what causes the seal is the air escaping from the jar and finding no way back in.

Then pressure can them at 10 pounds for 70 minutes (or follow your canner's instructions for green vegetables like broccoli or string beans).

It is important to pressure-can vegetables, unless they are pickled and/or have a high acidity like tomatoes and fruits or anything pickled. If you want to can your milkweed pods but don't have a pressure-canner, consider pickling them. There's a recipe in my first book (*Walking Away)* for hot pickled milkweed pods that is really a winner.

Make sure you've got a good seal (check the tops to make sure they are slightly concave) and store for winter.

7. LABYRINTHS
June 16, 2014

After a few months of cancelled plans, Mike and I finally decided to drive our twenty-year-old Honda civic down to Boston to see the girls. Our little car has some wonderful advantages: it gets excellent gas mileage, has a great stereo (with the aid of a makeshift wire antennae), and, after all these years, Mike understands its language of idiosyncratic rattles.

It also, however, has a broken engine fan. This last little bit is not a problem in Maine because, well, we just don't have any traffic. The engine gets wind-cooled. Taking it into one of the worst stop-and-go traffic labyrinths in the world is another story.

You might ask, why did they choose to take **that** car to Boston? Because, of all of the vehicles we have (and we have a few!), the little Honda, dubbed *Super Bunny,* was our best chance of getting us there. When you fix your cars yourself, you might have only one car working well at any given time. It's a little messy, but it keeps us moving.

If I wrote about all of the times Mike has fixed our car on the road with a flat-head screw driver and bungee cords, we would be here all day. As I have written in previous chapters, Mike knows the key to being able to fix cars (or anything), is to know how they work.

I guess that goes for fixing up human problems too. I heard myself telling my girls that I think, when we are born, we are dropped into our own personal labyrinths and are given no map, just people who sometimes take us deeper into the labyrinth and sometimes help us move out of it. While we are in it, though, we can't tell who is giving us the best advice. And, since it's cyclical, we keep moving in and out of layers as we travel through, revisiting places we have already been. It can be frustrating but, like the labyrinth of downtown Boston, there are many roads out, we just don't always recognize them.

Even if we think we know the way out for other people, they can only find their own way out. I also think the funny thing about labyrinths is that the best place is always right where we are. Even if it is not pleasant, it's where we can find meaning.

Some days we make good progress and other days we double back and lose hope. But we will all escape the labyrinth eventually. Until such time, we will just cycle in and out of our days of suns and moons. Each day is unique; each holds its lesson.

Our youngest daughter says she has always had an issue with change. It causes her anxiety. I understand because I have witnessed it many times as her mother, but I also find it humorous because, in the labyrinth, change is the only thing you can really count on. It is the only thing that doesn't.

Our faith waxes and wanes in almost predictable cycles, but we can't help but reflect the light of the sun most days. It's our nature to do so. We are all similes, masses of minerals held together impossibly by the gravitational pull of the sun. Eventually this attraction will create our symmetry. It might be a long process but it is warm in the sun. This little planet of the sun is where our matter is formed and what matters is formed. But growing is an individual thing and no one can do it for us.

Our eldest gets anxious when she has to show up for things. It's inexplicable, but as her mother, I also understand, since I have seen it in action many times before. She suffers from an inability to choose an outfit, leave the house in time to catch the bus or train, or find the meeting place. It's not always easy to show up for love.

Mike and I have learned that in the big picture, all our girls need is to know that we love them, whether they show up or not. Love fixes everything.

I used to tell my students at the end of the year, make sure you learn from other people's mistakes because there's no possible way you're going to be able to make all the mistakes you have to by yourself. Not everyone gets this on first try. It's okay. Eventually we all get it. It's written into every cell of the body. Our DNA is a spiraling, extended labyrinth of the impressions of people and places unique to us. It is our encoded ancestral memory. We learn from others or we circle around until we finally learn from ourselves, our older selves who have been this way before. Eventually we all learn what we came here to learn.

Even after our heated moments lost in the labyrinth of Boston traffic on a hot Father's Day in our little Honda with no engine fan, Mike and I were able to stay relatively cool. A few sparks flew when we realized that I had punched in the wrong address on the GPS and I had both girls on each of our cell phones at the same time. One of them was worried that we wouldn't make it and the other was worried she wouldn't make it.

But, in spite of all the human drama and an overheating car, we were able to find our way and we all met for a Father's Day lunch in Boston.

The fact that Mike was starving after a four-and-a-half-going-on-five hour drive on just one cup of coffee only added to the heat of the day. The fact that our kids took us to a cute little vegan restaurant where he ordered the *Bird's Nest Salad* added to the day's humor.

It gave him plenty to tease about later. "No man has ever in the history of the world said, *Oh no, I couldn't have dessert, that fake tofu-chicken Bird's Nest really stuck to my ribs.*"

Life would be no fun if there were *nothing* to complain about. Nevertheless, I wouldn't have missed that day for the world. I would gladly have spent hours circling past the same landmarks of my life for the joy that day brought me. Our girls seem to be setting strong feet on the paths of their own labyrinths of life.

And as for me, my feet also feel firmly planted on the Earth, finding their way past new territory and circling back through the familiar. Now I am able to take my time, survey the landscape, greet new friends, and ask directions.

I also have a wonderful travel companion who makes life interesting and fun, always willing to blaze new paths with me. Right now, we are two pilgrims travelling in an old car on a road to our divine location.

Someday, perhaps our paths will split again and I might have to know what it is like to pay a mechanic or he might have to share his meals with other folks at a restaurant counter. He'll probably be ordering endless plates with nothing green on them and telling the short-order cook about milkweed pods. I'll probably be sticking my head in the engine, offering the mechanic unschooled advice and arguing with him about his inflated quote.

But for now, I am happy to have him as a fellow traveler, sharing the days and nights, the moments of faith and faithlessness that inevitably accompany any life. In spite of our occasional breakdowns, I have faith that just about anything can be fixed. Mike can fix it, as long as it's an old car. He understands those.

URBAN FORAGING

Since eighty percent of the world's population lives in an urban or suburban setting, I like to think about the relevancy of my assertions in this series. But, once you start looking around you more, and noticing what is growing in the wild edges of backyards, ball fields and city parks, you might start exploring the uses of some of these weedy treasures. Always ask an expert. Don't just rely on internet pictures. And be mindful of what you harvest and where. There are more and more urban weed-walkers available every day and they are eager to share their knowledge. You might become one.

Make sure that your area is not a high traffic area or one that dogs "go" in. Lead content in soil is something to consider. Lead is most likely to be found where gas fumes collect (roadsides) and near the foundations of old homes (think lead house paint). But, as I pointed out in *Walking Away*, you might have to search for species in places like that to get to know them first. Once you recognize them, you can look for them in safer places. Don't forget to ask before taking if it is not public property. If it is public property, find out if they spray the area with insecticides or weed-killers.

Researchers have discovered that fruit trees absorb the least amount of lead from the soil. The amount of lead absorbed was greater in dark leafy greens, naturally. The research is still inconclusive, so make sure to do your own. Soil testing of your back yard or your local "spot" is a worthwhile endeavor. Most universities offer soil testing for free.

Some soil experts recommend adding elements to the soil to amend it, or adding new soil to raised beds. Again, a little research will help you find the best solution to your foraging needs in a city or suburban landscape.

Some plants you might find in an urban setting like Boston or New York might be the following.

If you are sure about its purity, plantain is edible both raw and cooked. You can also use it in salves by making an oil infusion (See Chapter 10). It grows everywhere, especially gravelly places like edges of parks. Bike paths usually are old railroad beds so, for the most part, they might be lead-free.

Other small leafy greens like lamb's quarters, wood sorrel, purslane (frog bellies), can be used to augment your salads in the summer. Think about flowers too. Bright orange daylilies are quite useful and look lovely in a salad. The yellow daylilies are a cultivar and are not edible, so, make sure you are getting the bright orange flowers. Just be really positive you know what you've got before you eat anything.

Dandelion is always a gem. If you read *Walking Away*, you know we use the leaves in salads, the flowers as fritters, and the roots in tea.

Other urban finds might be rose hips. We make a tasty and very nutritious fruit leather from rose hips. We soak them in a little water and cook them down (adding a little maple syrup or brown sugar for taste) and strain out the seeds to make a thick syrup. We then pour it into yoghurt container tops. We slip those onto the shelves of our dehydrator. Rose hips contain forty times more vitamin c than an orange!

Think about invasive plants like autumn olive and Japanese knotweed (the young shoots can be used like rhubarb and the roots are used to cure Lyme disease) when you start to look around. People almost never mind if you ask to take their weeds. Contrarily, berries and fruits are usually cultivated, so be sure to ask before you get out your pack baskets.

And remember, you can always cultivate your own edibles by taking plants from heavily-trafficked areas and transplanting them in a safer place of similar environment.

By controlling the soil, you may be able to have your own safe zone for your wild edibles. If left wild, a tiny raised bed could end up hosting a few favorites. Living in the city doesn't mean you can't forage. It just means that you may have to be smarter than your average bear. Have fun and be mindful. There's a whole world out there to discover.

8. WATER
June 26, 2014

It's raining today. I should write it's raining again today. It rains a lot up here. In fact, I think we live in a rainforest. The only difference is, it also snows a lot, but that's rain too, just frozen rain. I'm okay with that, though. My mind keeps repeating this little refrain I think I made up: *If you want to live in Maine, you'd best not complain.* People here comment on the weather, but they don't usually complain about it. The ones who do, move to Florida or have found a way to live there in the winter. You can tell right away who they are because they are unusually tan. And cheerful, I might add.

I'm not saying people around here aren't happy. They are. It's just about other things besides good weather. Bad weather, it turns out, is one of the reasons to live in these parts. For one thing, it guarantees that you'll only run into people who can muster up a good attitude about bad weather.

For another, there aren't too many of them. That means a lot less of all the bothersome types who whine about stuff you just can't control anyway. I happen to like that. A lot.

For another thing, an abundance of snow and rain creates places where nature has reclaimed water. That means that there's a bog, lake, brook, creek, stream, river, waterfall, or inlet just about everywhere you turn around here. Water, it turns out, is not a manmade concoction that is treated, stored, and piped into America's homes. It is its own entity, existing beyond man's control and, let's face it, in spite of his control.

Living on a river has given me a new appreciation for the thing that is more than ninety percent responsible for my being. I mean, I know my parents had something to do with it, but without water, I would be a pile of dusty things that don't hold together very well. There is a river that runs through me. I know because I hear about it in every other song on the radio. Being so close to the source of so much unbridled power is slowly wearing down the walls of my civic engineering, allowing my own rivers of creative expression to flow.

Around here, the rivers are curbed in few places. Otherwise, they are given their leeway. Farms exist in flood zones. Whatever topsoil might be lost, more seems to be gained, as the farms have continued on for centuries. House owners know what they are dealing with around here, and just deal with it. Men make codes and enforce setbacks but some of these grandfathered farmhouses are older than codes. They survive just fine, thank you.

Not that I'm saying people should build right on the river. I don't think they should. And most of them wouldn't anyway. Knowing the junk that goes into construction these days, I wouldn't want any of that in the river. Besides, we need the trees on the river banks to keep too much soil from washing downstream, preventing it from becoming an impossibly dirty place for fish to live.

If you like water, you'll probably need to like mud. People up here really look forward to Mud Season. It's an indication that winter is finally clearing out. It is time to get out the mud boards (various pieces of plywood that you save up to create little bridges out around your house). The black flies aren't out yet either so in its own little way, the mud means hope. Some people wait all year for mud season to arrive so they finally get that water-front property they always dreamed about.

Of course, getting your car stuck in the mud is prevalent up here. You might need to get someone to help you "yard-it-out," a common term in Maine for towing a car out of either snow or mud. Once when I dug the jeep in so far that it couldn't be yarded-out, Mike had to borrow a car jack from our friend Brian. The car's bumper was under mud. If you've ever sunk your foot in mud with a boot on, you'll know how difficult it is to release that suction. We had to dig into the mud to find a way to place the jack on the boards to get some kind of leverage. Then we had to dig out around the bumper for the other end of the jack. It took a while, but Mike finally got one tire free and that was all that was needed to free the rest.

Mud is what drew my friend Lyn and me together. We both love the kind of mud you throw on a wheel, bake at high temperatures, and then glaze in interesting ways. Yes, you guessed it, we are both pot-heads. Well, the innocent kind, anyway. She lives on the river too. We went to visit another pottery friend, an artist, Jemma, who lives on the same river, just twenty-eight miles closer to the source. Her studio is right on the edge of a falls. It is in a refurbished old garage that used to house Model T's.

"So, you're a water person too," she said to me not long after we met. Funny thing about artist types, they get straight to the essence of things. Especially potters. They are used to having their hand in the clay, the other less than ten percent that forms us. They understand the nature of having an idea in mind and then witnessing it become something even more lovely than what they had planned. Perhaps that is what we all could aspire to: making ourselves lovelier than our divine artist ever intended. Potters understand that the clay has a mind of its own. Sometimes the clay isn't willing or even interested in being lovely. Ultimately, it's the mud that determines the outcome. And, the truth is that too much water and too much fussing can ruin a good pot.

Water, especially running water, creates a space in our beings that connects us to all things. Like an open fire, it draws us to sit near, to listen to its tales of timelessness. It is security. Water cools our restless spirits, assuages our thirst for adventure, and provides the sustenance of our souls, clearing out the bottled up fears and worries of being human.

You may have heard of the Japanese Physicist Dr. Emoto (I didn't make this up, that's his real name.) who studied the effects emotional words and symbols have on water crystals. He photographed the crystals with an electron microscope and discovered that words like love, truth, and beauty created water crystals with symmetrical patterns that are absolutely startling in comparison with the chaotic and random shapes the crystals formed when exposed to negative words like hate, fear, and danger. After years of research, Dr. Emoto concluded that the words we use and think have a profound effect on the physical world (that's us). We are what we think. Water reminds us of the law of attraction.

Yes, I am a water person. I love the sound of the river rapids outside my bedroom window. I love that when feelings of worry and fear tug at me, I can sit on a river rock and rinse my mind of the negativity. I love the river and the ocean that it will become. I love the lakes, the mud, and the rain. Yes, I am a water person. And yes, I love the rain.

MITIGATING MOISTURE

I hope you don't have to deal with moisture in your basement. If you do, you know how disconcerting it can be. In our case, the moisture in the concrete foundation seeped up into the floor and walls of the house. We could never completely dry out and it took us quite a while to figure out what was going on.

At first, we thought it was the fact that we asked the guys who poured our foundation to build in a root cellar. We have not had a chance to vent it yet, so Mike boarded up the opening and we figured that we will get it going next year. He also tried insulating the floor joists from underneath, keeping the bulkhead doors open during the day in the summer. This backfired too often when it down-poured unexpectedly. We also ran a fan in the worst spots 24-7.

The moisture content of the basement decreased slightly after all of these measures. At least we could control the humidity in the guest bedroom enough to consider putting a floor in. But, it still remained a problem until Mike decided to think about what was going on outside.

His first measure was to fill in a depression in the landscape that had formed right around the bulkhead. When it rained, he discovered, the water pooled in that area and was seeping into the concrete foundation.

After reading on-line about how much water an average roof sheds per minute when it rains (something like 1000 gallons), he decided that we needed to install some gutters. The gutters direct the water to a spot far away from the foundation.

Most people hire someone to put up gutters because leveling them can be a little tricky. Most people don't build their own homes, either.

Fortunately, Mike researched all of the pitfalls of installing your own gutters and was able to get it done himself in record time. Mike attached three-inch PVC to the end of the gutter to send the water far away from the house. It worked. Our basement is now dry as a bone. I can't help but have faith in Mike since he always seems to be able to mitigate any problem that surfaces. In this case, the problem was sinking.

9. AIR
August 22, 2014

I have discovered that everything works better when you expose it to a little air. While building the house, I was in charge of the materials. This summer, I discovered that the pine finish-wood for our window casings and floor molding that I had carefully moved and double-tarped in June had created a perfect incubator for mildew. Without air, the boards were stained grey and black.

When I discovered the mildew, I was devastated. We just don't have the money to replace a pallet of one-by pine finished board. After a few deep breaths, I decided I had better try consulting an expert. That day we ran into a contractor we had worked with on a job and asked him. His remedy worked. Any mark can be cleared with some air, sunshine, a little dishwasher soap and bleach. It took time to scrub the 500-600 feet of board, but it was worth it.

I had to laugh at myself because if I had just left the pallet the way it was, all messy and spread out, rather than work so hard to wrap it up in a tight little bundle, I would have avoided the mildew altogether.

Effort, I am discovering, is not as important as breathing. I knew this from my yoga practice. Now I know it from building a house.

Aside from being important in avoiding mildew, air is one of the most important design features in a home. It is the ultimate insulator. Simply by installing two-inch strapping between the four inches of insulation (filled with air pockets) and the plywood sheathing, creating space in the roof for air, we have increased our R-factor considerably. Our house is designed with the same feature for the walls. Even though our house is a cedar log cabin, the interior walls contain a sandwich of ½ inch insulation, one-inch strapping, and cedar tongue and groove. Standing inside, you can't tell the walls are insulated but it cuts down on feeding the wood stove in the winter and is cool in the summer.

Though our insulation package cost us a little more, it gave us the ability to harness the power of something that is still free, the most valuable thing on earth: air.

When Mike and I talk about the shift we are making, we very often refer to the fact that we are just trying to keep things simple. In my mind, there's nothing simpler than the need for good clean air to breathe.

The need for clean air is personal to me. I was born in Los Angeles. My father, the son of tropical winds, decided he could not raise me there. He says he just couldn't breathe the air. So, at the age of six weeks, I was on a cross-country train ride with my parents and my brother, on our way to a different destiny to Central Florida where there are still lots of trees. The imprint of my first months of breathing on my own has patterned in me the soul of a traveler, constantly in search of fresh air.

While I write, my musical accompaniment is the sound of the wind in the trees. It is telling me that it will be an early winter and I must gather and prepare as much as I can in the next few weeks. The hummingbirds are feeding heavily, preparing their flight. The bees aren't as active as they normally are during the goldenrod bloom. All beings are listening to the uncharacteristically cool air to tell them what is up. Their life's hymns will be watchful and steady. My own hymn finds harmony with theirs.

And though my first response might be to stay inside to avoid the chill of the morning wind, I can't resist the need for new air, the kind that is filtered through millions of trees. Like the boards that I covered up a little too well, I could easily become a place where dark moldy ideas and moods find a home. I am better for exposing myself to the sun and air, allowing for a little bit of disheveling. Too much effort, too much careful wrapping, can be counterproductive. It allows for no flow.

When involved in a conversation, I think it is always better when we breathe. That allows us to listen more than talk. Talking is breath interrupted. It's pretty simple. Talk less. Breathe more. The wisdom of age teaches us that.

Traditional practitioners of yoga believe that we are born with an allotted number of breaths. They recommend taking each one as a separate moment to savor and cherish. As it turns out, when we slow our breathing, our lungs are better able to process the air and the blood is able to absorb the oxygen we take in. Slower, deeper breaths also allow the lungs to expel the waste products it produces (carbon dioxide) more efficiently. More oxygen in the blood means better overall health and clearer thinking.

Somewhere tucked away in all of our psyches is a tiny message, like a little white strip of wisdom that gets baked into a fortune cookie. The fortune for our lives: You must never settle for anything but good clean air.

That need for clean air has been given a name in some cultures. It is called "forest bathing" or *shinrin-yoku* in Japan and is a medical prescription to boost the immune system, lower blood pressure, increase energy levels, the ability to sleep, and focus for children.

The Norwegians enjoy a similar idea, *firluftsliv*, literally translated as "free air life." The idea here is that all humans need a little fresh air sometimes. A walk out in nature is obviously good for the body. The Norwegians know it is also good for the mind and spirit too. They even incorporate it into some of their school curricula. It is only a matter of time before the importance of getting fresh air breathes new life into our school curricula.

As it turns out, keeping things all secured in a tight little bundle might not be the best thing for anyone. Having fresh air means providing space for plants to grow too. In spite of some efforts at marketing oxygen bars in the big cities, nothing can replace a walk through a forest or by the ocean.

My objective for wrapping the trim wood up so tight was to protect it from the elements. I did not realize that all of my efforts would cause such failure. Even though I was able to rescue most of the boards by exposing them to a bleach solution, sunshine, and a lot of fresh air, I lost many boards to deep staining. I would have been much better served to keep the boards a little untamed on their pallet. The fresh air would have done them some good.

DEHYDRATING FOOD

Living off-grid means being creative with your food storage. I used to be able to freeze anything I wanted in large quantities because I had a freezer chest in my basement. Though I still use that chest freezer in the winter on our front porch, it is not available during the end of summer when I need it most. My year-round freezer space is now approximately one-and-a-half cubic feet. Our refrigerator is run on propane and it is much smaller than your average family refrigerator.

Canning vegetables is fine but changes the texture and color considerably since you have to pressure can vegetables for seventy minutes at ten pounds. That means that they get mushy and I'm not sure how much nutritional value is conserved that way. I still can things like string beans, milkweed pods, and turnips.

The best way to store leafy greens, I have discovered, is to dehydrate them. You can fit five or six good, hearty bunches of kale, spinach, Swiss chard, and beet greens in one half-gallon ball jar. It's amazing. I also fit close to fifteen pounds of broccoli in the same sized ball jar this summer.

The color and texture are completely preserved. I also find that it is really easy to use the leafy vegetables this way. I just throw a handful into my soups. I crumble them in my hands before I throw them in if I want them chopped.

The most important reason to dehydrate vegetables is that it preserves ninety percent of the plant's nutrients.

The other side of living off-grid is that a dehydrator draws a ton of power so it has to be done during sunny summer days. That means that most fall fruits must be dehydrated really early in the fruit season. We like to make fruit leathers in the dehydrator. But, tomato leathers are a good thing to make if you run out of jars and need to set up some tomato paste. You can take the skins and cores of the tomatoes you have canned and dry them for stock.

Also, if you happen to get a lot of bear one day (see chapter thirteen), you can use your dehydrator to make some jerky that will stay fine on a shelf. Just season well with a dry rub or marinate in spices since salt, pepper, herbs, and spices are all natural preservatives.

10. SPIDER MEDICINE
September 9, 2014

Two weeks ago, while stacking firewood for a friend, I felt a sharp sting on my left hip just under the waistband of my khaki shorts. I didn't think much of it. It was a hot day and there are always insects in firewood. When I got home that night, I discovered a little red bump that I was sure was the result of a spider bite. No big deal, I thought. But, after a few days, the red bump got progressively larger and the skin around it was red, hot, and hard. Mike and I googled the symptoms and came up with what seemed very much like a nasty boil.

"I've got the pox!" I ran around joking. It was bothersome so I took it seriously, and used a few different homemade remedies, including an onion poultice with turmeric on it, then I resorted to an over-the-counter drawing salve with a sulfur base and thick waxy consistency. Now, if you're the queasy type, you may want to turn to a different chapter or skip to the middle of this one.

After a week of watching my "boil" get worse and witnessing a strangely wide opening at the top, Mike demanded that we go to the emergency room and get it looked at. His google search led him to some interesting pictures. They were so disconcerting to him that he didn't want to show me. I agreed readily.

That morning I had shown my "boil" to Grandfather Isaac, an elder herbalist. I was a little impressed by his wide-eyed expression when, after telling me the story of cutting his knee straight to the bone and how he healed it with plantain and comfrey, he said, "Oh boy, I've never seen anything that bad before."

A week after I felt that sharp pain while stacking wood, I heeded my husband's urging and went to the hospital. The truth is, I had been in a lot of pain and didn't realize it until I put Grandfather Isaac's plantain and comfrey salve on the "boil" and the pain finally ceased. When you're busy, you don't always pay attention to pain, even though you're feeling it. I am pretty sold on both plantain and comfrey for repairing skin wounds and helping with pain.

"Oh, yah," said Dr. Scott, "This looks like a spider bite alright. Brown recluse, I'd say." He seemed so matter of fact about it even though Maine isn't supposed have brown recluse spiders. "See the necrosis? That's where the venom kills your skin cells and it will keep spreading." He and Mike were examining my side. Fortunately, I can't really see it that well because of its location. "Yup, pretty ugly. But you're lucky you are so healthy because it has been a week and it's pretty contained. Keep an eye on it to make sure the area doesn't grow in size. If it does, come back in right away."

He put me on an antibacterial IV and after stabbing the area of the wound with a five inch needle (a lot like a railroad spike) to numb the pain, he scraped it out. Not even the plantain could keep me from digging my nails into the metal gurney. Funny thing is, I discovered that I am allergic to whatever he gave me for pain and began to itch like a meth addict. I was scratching uncontrollably at my scalp until the nurse came in and jabbed an Epi-pen into my left thigh and hooked up a second bag to my IV.

After a few hours, I was all geared up with oral and topical antibiotics (the strongest they make) and sent home to attend to my spider bite on my own, carefully avoiding Googling pictures of brown recluse spider bites. I was told some people have lost massive areas of skin to necrosis. It is much like a burn where doctors must graft skin where the skin cells have died as a result of the venom. Mine is only the size of a quarter. I am grateful. It will heal.

This is where you can come back into the story if you can't take gross stuff.

Being an all-time believer that things happen for a reason, especially things that force us to pause a minute and slow us down (usually illness does this), I ask what the meaning of it all is. The truth is that for the last month or so, I have been running into spider webs and finding spiders in my path on a daily basis. I ask myself, "What does this mean? What is spider trying to tell me?" *Is it to stop wearing that fly perfume?* I understand now that spiders were trying to get my attention in subtle ways but I wasn't paying attention so they had to shout a little louder.

I have come to learn that every time I do not stop to pay attention to my inner truth, I decrease my aliveness. Being too busy can get in the way of fully being present. Our bodies react to the business with numbness, pain, and a loss of vitality which leaves openings for all kinds of afflictions. When we trust our intuition and slow down enough to notice the signs along the way, sinking into our awareness, we allow the energy of the universe to move through us and we feel fully alive. This aliveness creates a luminous egg around us that keeps the pesky stuff from being attracted to us. It's kind of like keeping a clean house. When there's less stuff around for bugs to eat, there are less bugs.

Housekeeping and keeping our luminous egg intact are related. You could spend an entire day sweeping, dusting, and organizing your house and in comes another person and drops shoes, tools, and laundry in a swath of destruction through your day of peaceful order. That happens with our peaceful eggs too. I have found it best just to laugh and ask that person to kindly remove the crud but that's not always a harmonious enterprise, especially if the person is tired and cranky and you're all relaxed because you weren't "busy" that day. It is really funny when you stop to think about it.

The luminous egg is like that too. You're enjoying a meditative moment, listening to your inner voice, and your housemate turns up the news to be able to hear it better. It's just that way. So, how do you deal? Anger only leads to resentment, and more anger over completely unrelated things. Letting it go and just picking up the mess leads to more resentment. You could decide to live alone but it won't have cured what you need to work on which is how to communicate your needs without inciting disharmony.

Of course, if the house is clean and organized, asking the person to pick up a personal mess is more reasonable and frankly easier to execute. It may even create an environment where that person wouldn't think of leaving laundry in the living area. Who knows?

So what does spider tell us about life? What has it been trying to tell me? To stop flailing around wildly in the sticky web of life, let go, and walk lightly, so as to avoid entanglement. In short, be the spider, not the fly.

My good friend, Michael Douglas once told me, "It is better to be the hero in your own story than the victim in someone else's."

When you are the spider, you can discard any web you have created at any time and can create a new web, an intentional web. And if that web is damaged by another person inadvertently walking through who doesn't notice your beautiful creation, you are free to create a new web.

Recovering from the brown recluse bite has forced me to slow down and rest. My body is sending all of its resources to my left side to repair the damaged skin. There is a hole in my shield that I must be careful to protect while the miraculous cells of my organism engineer the correct and sane way to close it up. We all know that patches, the quick fix, will only seal in the toxic substances. The body knows that it is better to take time and heal from the inside out.

So, I am spending time sitting by the river with Hermes who eases my angst as only dogs can. He actively runs along its shore trying to catch crawfish while I sit still. I absorb the warmth of the sun from above and the warmth of the rock from below. The river has a way of pulling things out of my deepest places and I cry. I shed the last tear I ever need to shed for my past and whatever sticky web it created to keep me from being fully present in my new web. I am wrapping up the old web, full of all kinds of stuff I no longer need, and sending it all downriver to travel its journey out to sea where all things are cured in its salt.

And today I ruminate on the importance of being the spider, not the fly. I dance around my house to music and clear the dusty clutter from under my bed. I resolve to take rest seriously and perhaps read an inspiring book to deepen my understanding. I allow myself time to spin my tales and to sort through the geometrics of living life beautifully.

The wound in my side is healing. But more importantly, my heart is healing. I no longer trust like a child does. Yet, because of my experience, I trust that I can fold up any web of life at any time and create a new one.

I am not afraid of any ole spider. I am the spider!

MAKING SALVES

When you find a plant that works for you or would like to experiment with its leaves or flowers in a topical application, try making an oil infusion. The only limit is your imagination.

According to John Greene, author of the leading book on herbal preparations, *The Herbal Medicine Maker's Handbook,* the best oils for infusions are olive oil and peanut oil.

To infuse your liquid oils, place your dried herb in a glass jar with a lid. You will want to try and put as much into a jar as you can. Then add the oil and let the mixture sit in a warm place (90-110 degrees F) for about ten days, shaking the jar a few times a day. Make sure you strain out every bit of the herb to keep your oil infusion pure.

To make a salve, you can add melted beeswax and a solid oil like Shea butter or coconut oil. Some people use tallow. Think about the properties of your oils when you choose them. Virgin organic Shea butter and coconut oil have their own curative properties for skin.

If you want to make your salve soft and smooth, use less beeswax. Add more if you want it to hold up longer. The ratio is about 1 cup oil to 1/8 cup beeswax. Add equal amounts of solid oil to liquid oil. (This is a rough estimation so you might need to experiment.)

Never heat oils directly on the heat source. Always use a double boiler or simply place the ring of a ball jar at the bottom of your pot of simmering water (to create an easy rack) and place the canning jar filled with the oils on its ring.

Once you get the idea with one plant, you can begin to mix your infusions, based on their properties. I also add store-bought essential oils to my salves sometimes. The first thing anyone does when they open a salve is to smell it. That's because nature designed our olfactory sense to dominate our testing abilities. If it smells bad, it is bad. Possible plants for salves include: rosemary, plantain, comfrey, jewelweed, lavender, chamomile, St. John's wort, and any others that I forgot or I might not know about. Possible essential oils are lavender, tea tree, rosemary, calendula, and possibly a combination of these.

Think about keeping your salves in an airtight and light-repellent jar (preferably glass). Store in a cool place out of the sun. If you need to refill a smaller jar from your large jar, just heat it up in hot water in a double boiler (or use your ring-rack), but don't heat above 110 degrees.

11. EARTH
September 13, 2014

Even though I am not going back to school, September is the busiest time of the year. My to-do list is a little different than it used to be but the pressures are similar. Youthful vigor will not wait for a teacher who has procrastinated planning lessons or correcting quizzes and papers. The Earth will not wait for the forager who procrastinates picking ripe elderberry and blackberry, collecting goldenrod and the last of the leafy wonders like plantain. In fact, I have been so busy the last few weeks that my to-do list takes up two sides of a sticky note. It is time to dust powdered sugar over the bees to control mites, set up some bread kits so bread-making is easier, make muesli (our morning cereal) since we're out, roast up some coffee beans so I can grind them, bottle up some of the shrugs I set up and store them in the cellar, call the "bee man" about purchasing his equipment, make a bread, make elderberry jam, sand the spindles Mike is using to finish up the deck rails, cook up a chicken and barley soup, bake oatmeal cookies to take to the neighbor who invited us over, clear the one-by finish planks off the deck, oh yah, rearrange space in the basement so they can be stored down there until we get to them, practice some yoga, and as always, write. After looking at my list, Mike comments that I should also run for governor in my spare time.

I didn't get to the writing like I should have, since that is my primary reason for doing all of the rest of it. But, I wrote in my head as I worked as efficiently as possible in my makeshift kitchen to make sure I store up as much of nature's bounty as possible. I also need to maximize the dry goods we purchase in town to keep us well-fed on a low budget. Sure, you might be able to purchase elderberry jam and homemade bread in a high-end deli but it won't be nearly as fresh. In addition, it would be expensive. Even in our old lives of good salaries it would have only been an occasional treat, to be sure.

Mike and I intend to finish up the exterior of the house so we don't end up living in it with a host of incomplete projects. Nothing, I have found, causes stress like unfinished business. And right now, there's a lot of it!

Yesterday Mike left for work at six in the morning to install someone's solar system in Monson and got home around 2:00. When he got home, he fixed the seal on the front door and finished the last three sections of the deck railing. When that was done, we got ready to go to Larry's for dinner and some fireworks. Larry's helping us with our kitchen cabinets. We now have the cabinets we need to install our kitchen island/dining room table. We decided to use old slate roof shingles for our countertops tops. Slate is tough as nails and impenetrable. Old roof shingles are pretty easy to get up here and are extremely economical. With a few good coats of tile sealer, it looks pretty slick.

There's a lot going on here. We are busy, that's for sure, but it is all a fun-kind of busy. Who minds a long list of things that must get done when they include items like berry-picking? Our life is filled with a five-day weekend and two days of "work". We work on building the house this year but next spring our list will include a wood/tool shed and, eventually, a small tree house for guests to stay in that can be also used as my personal office and yoga studio.

We don't have jobs in the common use of the word, but we work all the time. The funny thing is that we don't mind the work. It is not stressful, it is satisfying, because we actually enjoy the full benefits of whatever we accomplish. Our pay is full satisfaction of a delicious, healthy meal and a clear, spacious porch area with an amazing railing that will hold up a lot longer than either of us will. We build and write for our heirs, taking the chance that there will be some, that they will appreciate the written records, the land, and the house.

We take the chance that the house will not be threatened by any destructive elements. But these are the risks we are content taking. Each day now is dedicated to something that will outlive us if we're lucky.

When I was a teacher, my students' essays had to make it back to the kids in a timely manner. If not, I would have to deal with their excuses for handing them in late the next time, wasting precious learning time. Even though procrastination is universally human, if you want your students to take you seriously, you have to try to be a little better than that. The truth is, if we all give in to procrastination, we will all end up wasting precious time.

With an Earth-based lifestyle, the pressure is a little different: all of the elderberries don't really have to be cleaned and dropped into the pot. But, who could stand the waste if they weren't?

Then, there's the fact that we are here to be a part of nature, not apart from it. That means we must take time to be outside and witness the Earth's changes. September is the time for wrapping up, gathering mushrooms, drying herbs, digging potatoes, and processing Earth's bounties from the garden. Appreciating the Earth's abundances are just as much about being outside enjoying the earthy smell of mushrooms while we try to locate deer paths through the woods as it is about setting up elderberry syrup and jam.

At some point, the to-do list will be shorter. That's when Mike and I will make some coffee, toast up a piece of homemade bread, crack open an elderberry jam, and settle back into a warm bed to work on a puzzle. By then, our railings for the deck will all be up, the kitchen cabinets will all be in place, the countertops will be done, the bees will be safely tucked into their insulated boxes, all healthy and mite-free, and we will just cozily watch the snow fall.

MUESLI

Eating muesli is something that is common in Europe but not as common for Americans. I'm not sure why Americans prefer to cook their oats but I happen to love eating mine raw. My oats are never plain. They are always mixed with dried fruits, nuts, and topped with fresh honey and raw milk.

At this point in time, most of the dried fruits I mix in are fruits I have gathered and dried myself in a dehydrator. The nuts and seeds (sunflower, pumpkin, chia, and sesame) come from stores and I gather them whenever I come across a good deal somewhere. This year I will be planting some American filbert (hazelnut) seedlings in the spring. It will take a few years, but judging by the way we eat muesli, I think Mike and I will both be around to harvest them.

Why eat muesli? Oats you normally buy are much older than they would be if you grew the oats yourself or bought them locally. That means that the oils in the grains are older too. Cooking the oats reduces their nutritional value even more. Rolling your own oats from groats is undeniably the best way to go but requires a hand-operated roller that we don't have yet. Whether the oats are fresh or not, raw oats are undeniably good fiber and act as an efficient cleanser for the digestive tract. There is much talk recently about phytates and phytase. Phytates are called an anti-nutrient. Plants use them to discourage us from eating them. It is a defense mechanism. Phytase is the micronutrient that allows the body to absorb the nutrients of the plant or its seeds. We mix some rye flakes in with our oats to add the phytase to help our bodies absorb all of the wonderful benefits of eating oats.

Dried fruits and nuts add their own nutrition to our muesli, including protein and essential fatty acids. There is much talk about phytates in these as well so some people soak their oats to aid in the absorption of nutrients.

I go by how I feel. My body is able to discard its wastes efficiently when I eat muesli regularly. When I add my own honey and some raw milk, I am confident that I have a nutritional meal that keeps me going all day long with a long, slow burn.

It is the ultimate breakfast.

12. MOTHER HEALING
October 8, 2014

Mothering is a lot like writing. You start a chapter, not really sure where it's going, but you do your best and just go with it. The only difference is that life doesn't give us a delete button on mothering. Any mistakes, neglectful moments, or too much attention go down in the annals of history. Fortunately, nature has given us forgetfulness and a mind that is prone to editing its stories.

When we scan back on our life experiences, we want a beginning, middle and an end. We want a moral to a story or some nugget of meaning to take away like a doggy bag from a fancy restaurant. We want a theme. We want an entrée with side dishes that go with it. But life isn't always a narrative. It's usually an unsolved mystery with loads of clues and evidence that doesn't add up to anything discernable. It just is. Sometimes it's pasta and potatoes in the same white Styrofoam clamshell.

When Mike and I married, the girls were in their tweens. They were too young to stay home alone, then quickly became too old. On our much-cherished date-nights, we got in the habit of asking the waiter from our favorite restaurant to write things like "fish and anchovies" on the tops of our little white boxes so when the kids found them in the fridge, they wouldn't even attempt to open them. We had tired of finding our carefully saved lobster-stuffed grouper filets and eggplant parmesan pilfered by our kids.

One time, Mike had saved a rack of ribs and mashed potatoes to eat at work the next day. He had been talking about them all morning to the other guys on the job. When it came time to open up the little white box and have at it, what he found was a three-day-old Mexican omelet that was surely regurgitated. Our eldest daughter had switched out leftovers.

Even a life without kids is full of surprises like that. Having kids just gives us a little more material when it comes to that kind of stuff.

They provide us with the kinds of stories I like to remember. The ones that make me laugh are the valuable ones. The ones that make me want to cry creep in and knock at my psyche in the middle of the night or they sneak in as dreams and before I know it, I'm dreaming that I'm driving in a car with one of my kids, desperately trying to find the other one. The one in the seat next to me is the one who is talking to me right now. I mean, she's the one who will answer my text messages. She is growing up, I think to myself, as I sit in the passenger seat of the two-seater car. Dreams sometimes make more sense than our waking life. But often dreams tell stories about things that don't make us laugh, at least not right away.

One thing I have always loved about my mother's family is that they find a way to laugh about the most painful things. Somehow, if you can do that, life isn't so hard. Through our laughter and storytelling, we smooth out the pain, like wrinkles in our favorite dress; after the disaster, we smooth out our appearance, stand up straight, and are ready to face the world with a clear face.

Everyone makes mistakes; some mistakes are harder to face than others. The point is, when we wake up, when we realize it was a mistake, do we get up, straighten ourselves out, and then walk out of it? Or do we sit there in a wrinkled mess, with runny make-up, complaining about how tough we have it?

Heroes are people who can find their feet.

One of the things I love about Mike is that he feels gratitude for blessings yet to come. He says that's what he loves most about me (that and my baked beans). They both are good for a little chuckle on occasion. That's not to say that we have not had our share of dark moments. But being willing to sort it out is not only good for us; it's good for our kids. When the kids see us able to communicate and laugh together, it gives them a sense of stability. Maybe some of the instability they experienced growing up can be remedied by what they witness today as they move into adulthood.

They will come to visit us in the house that love built. Love gives us the reason to give a person another chance, to allow them to rewrite the endings of their stories; to be the hero. Love is our only mission while we are here. We go to school and we think that we have to be a leader in some way or make a difference in some field. The truth is, we go to school to love life more deeply, know and love ourselves more fully, and to feel solid in our relationships. We cultivate ourselves so we are able to recognize love when it shows up in the bright eyes of a friend. The truth is, life is a school. We don't have to worry about missing the registration date. The most successful people in life are people who are free to love with all their hearts.

When I think of my own mother, I think of how I must have put her through so much torture but she still loves me. An awesome truth. My mother taught me the power of love. It is not something that just edits the ending of our stories, it is a subscript to everything we do, a whisper behind the narrative that says, "It's okay, baby, you're going to make mistakes, sometimes pretty ugly ones. It's okay, you can't help but be human. Trouble will find you. But I love you and that will never change."

Love doesn't always come in the form of our human mothers. Like the Japanese and the Norwegians, Americans know that nature heals us. The more time we spend with Mother Nature, the more we realize how forgiving and loving she is. She heals herself from the wounds her children inflict on her. Her love is so vast that it supersedes any human love.

Part of our healing here, as humans, is to reconcile our relationships with Nature. Can we find it in our hearts to take the gifts she so freely offers, her humble gifts, not the ones we wish she would give us? Can we accept the gifts of a simple herb that grows through our graveled expanses, places we create to shut her out! We try so hard to keep her out through the poison sprays and mechanical blades. Can we stoop low to recognize the amazing beauty and power of her simple weeds and say, "Thank you Mother!" She knows what we need and places it before us every day. We don't have to live in the woods to know her and receive her gifts; we only need to go back to a different school of thought, a school where love rules, a school where the motto is "Love your mother and father and each other."

She has been there, watching, through all of human existence, while the aborigines used poison to catch their river fish, while the industrialists pumped oily smoke into the air, while we engineered the perfect wheat plant that makes a large, fluffy loaf of bread but makes people sick.

In her wisdom, our mother knows that, eventually, when we get sick enough, we will learn our lessons, and we will turn back to her and seek her loving arms and her simple gifts.

Like our mothers, she doesn't want us to hang our heads in shame. What she really wants is to be able to look into the shiny eyes of a friend and see love there. It's just that simple.

BREAD KITS

Living off-grid and making most of your own stuff doesn't necessarily mean that you have to give up modern expediencies like ready-made convenience foods. It just means that you make them yourself. It is cheaper and the quality is infinitely better. If you talk to some families who live self-sufficient lifestyles, they will recommend that your grain be stored whole, and then ground as it is used, for full nutritional absorption.

I am prepared to take it to that level and probably will start to do so this winter, but in the meantime, I would like to share what I have done in the past to make my life easier in the kitchen.

We discovered long ago that store-bought bread just doesn't live up to our expectations unless we paid more for it than we were able. That's when we researched the best bread machine on the market, bought it, and began setting up our own bread kits. The best time to experience fresh-baked bread, warm, and ready to eat, is in the early morning. (Monday is best.) With a bread machine, you can put all of your ingredients into the pan the night before and set the timer for when you would like to wake up to the smell of fresh-baked bread. It's the best alarm clock.

I don't use my bread machine in the winter because it draws a lot of power from our solar array and we don't collect as much in the winter. But, even if I could, I wouldn't, because I prefer the crusty feel of hand-kneaded bread and the irregularity of shape I get from the bread pan or pizza stone I use.

The recipe is easy. Just put all of your dry ingredients except the yeast into a zip-lock bag. Write the wet ingredients on the bag, including quantities, of course.

I use this method for things I make often like pies, scones, and cookies. You would be surprised at how easy it makes baking. I don't have to get out several different bins and measuring cups each time I get ready to bake. One bowl and a spot for kneading dough is all I need.

I usually set up between seven and twelve kits, depending on the frequency of use. You never know when you need to whip up a quick batch of blueberry scones for someone who has done something good for you. In less than twenty minutes you can have an impressive thank-you warm and ready. If it is a huge favor, add a little homemade jam and place it in a small box lined with a napkin, and you've said thank you like nothing else can. Now that's preparing for blessings yet to come!

13. UNCANNY LIFE
November 12, 2014

I canned up a bunch of rutabagas yesterday and my house still smells funny. The three hours I spent in my kitchen was worth it just to be able to say that to the other students in my pottery class. The whole conversation went something like this:

"So, what kind of handle do you think I should put on this teapot?"

"I don't know. That one looks a little awkward and hard to use. Try making it a little shorter."

"I canned up a lot of rutabagas today. My house still smells like farts."

(Insert deadpan silence here.)

The truth is, I am used to being a little odd. I'm comfortable with it. Their silence told me right away that my pottery friends are not canners. In the company of canners, that comment might have been met with an enthusiastic, "So, where did you get your rutabagas?" That would be all I needed to tell a great story (at least in my mind).

Some people can; I'm not talking about your hobbyist who goes out and buys strawberries at the grocery store and cooks up some strawberry jam to impress coworkers at Christmas. (Anyway, that's how I started.) I'm talking about the people who happen to come across a ton of something and they would rather find a way to preserve it than to let it go to waste or go to someone else. That's what happened with the rutabaga.

I stopped by Isaiah's farm on my way home from work to pick up some acorn squash since he had a sign out front that read, "Squash 50 cents a pound – self-serve." Since Mike and I designed a root cellar into the plans of our house, we can store a twenty-pound sack of winter squash without much waste. I love to hollow them out and stuff them for individual servings.

Isaiah's squash are small and perfect for my recipe. To truly appreciate this story, you need to know that Isaiah is the minister of the Baptist church right down the road from his house. I imagine he is in his mid-seventies but his open, unassuming gaze belies his age. He could just as easily be ten.

When Mike and I first met Isaiah, he told us that he was one of seven children in a poor household where his father was an aggressive alcoholic. (Around here it's totally normal for people to openly recount their life's stories to perfect strangers on first meeting. It breaks the ice, if you know what I mean.)

I weighed out about twelve of the little green squash, loaded them into my sack, and placed my $15.00 under the rock in the Tupperware container. As I was doing this, I noticed sounds of tinkering coming from the barn. I figured that if it was the minister, I could extend the gratitude I felt for his squash since anywhere else I would be paying twice as much.

There he was, sitting at a makeshift table with a cutting board and a cleaver, peeling squash and tossing the little orange chunks in a cardboard box next to the table.

Isaiah doesn't know me. I know him. But he greeted me as if he did. "Hi there! I'm just peeling these up for a friend who can't peel them. I've got so many of them, see. God has been really good to us this year."

If there's one thing I have learned from Isaiah, it's that being wealthy is never about what you own, it's about what you give. And he's a pretty wealthy guy.

"Well, Pastor, I just wanted to pass along my gratitude for your squash. It's really nice of you to sell them at such a good price. My husband loves it when I stuff them and bake them."

"Come here, I want to show you something."

Doing so required that I follow him into a really dark part of the barn, down some steps, and through a creepy old door. He still had the cleaver in his hand and the daylight was closing in. If the pastor's intention was to get me to pray, it worked.

A few moments later, Isaiah threw on a switch and the whole place lit up. It was a root cellar he just finished digging for his turnips. There was a whole crop of them. Some were the size of basketballs. Most were sprouting light green and purple leaves from their tops. They all were coated in dirt.

"Will you do me a favor?"

"Sure, what do you need?" I'm figuring that he needs some help lifting something or moving turnips from the root cellar to the front of the barn for sale.

"Would you take some of these turnips? I have so many, see. These here, see, they're rutabagas. That's the best tasting kind of turnip you can get."

"Well, I'll take one since you offered. Thank you very much. You're quite generous."

"No, you have to take more." The pastor began to load up a sack he was carrying. He would not stop loading me up with turnips, no matter how much I objected. After I realized the futility of my protests, I saw the beauty of his ways. "These are a little soft on top but you can cut that part out, see."

"Yes, sir, I do see. In fact, I'm going to take them home tonight and can them up. My husband loves turnips and so do I. Thank you very much."

So, when I walk downstairs with twelve quart jars filled to the top with chunks of the golden, earthy goodness, I feel rich. If you can, you know how precious that moment is when you take empty jars, fill them up with something that cost you little more than being appreciative, and you place them on your shelves to enjoy during the winter months. It truly is a blessing. It's a little reminder that being rich is about what you give in life. It's also a great story if anyone happens to ask you why your house smells like farts.

CANNING MEAT

If your life is anything like ours, you never know when your neighborhood hunting guide will show up with a couple of legs of bear to give you. When it happens, you have to be ready to move your cans!

Before we begin, there's a very important thing to remember about canning and it is that unless what you're canning is really high in acid like a vinegar pickle, tomato sauce, or fruit jam, you have to pressure can it. The problem with putting up food is that the natural bacterium, Clostridium botulinum, is present in all foods but its growth is arrested by acidity, extreme heat, or extreme cold. Botulism is no joking matter. It can kill you.

Meat of any kind has to be pressure canned if you are not going to freeze it. We have found that it is best to braise the meat a little beforehand with some seasonings to make a good stew or pot pie or anything else you would make with meat.

If you manage with a little less like us, you may be interested in canning your meat when it is on sale at the grocery store. We typically can up turkey around Thanksgiving and pork when those large loins are on sale. It is not the same as wild meat, but in a cold climate, it can be the basis of a pie, soup, or stew without much effort.

We always boil the bones with vegetable scraps, fresh herbs, salt, and pepper to make a good broth. Try to skim off some of the fat that rises to the top of the broth when it cools to help the tops seal well. The fat from the broth can grease up the seals and keep your jars from sealing properly. But, no need to get too fixated on the fat. A little cider vinegar on a paper towel to wipe the edge can take care of that. The clear gelatin that accumulates when the broth cools is good stuff. Don't get rid of it.

Most recipes call for 90 minutes of pressure canning for meat. As always, make sure they're sealed before storing.

If you think you might pressure-can, Mike and I recommend that you look into the All American Canner because it has no rubber seal. When the rubber seal gets a little worn, it stretches and won't create a good seal. If you use a traditional pressure canner, make sure the seal is in good working order.

Any pressure cooker can be used as a canner as long as you use the rack that usually comes with it or you devise a rack system. An easy solution is to use the rings from canning jars to line the bottom of the pot just as you would with a makeshift water canner. Most pressure canners only require two-to-three inches of water. Follow the instructions that come with your canner or find them online. Also, make sure you use canning jars.

14. GIFTS
December 15, 2014

I live for those little white slips in a fortune cookie. The messages attached to a tea bag, the roadside pulpits and bumper stickers can often sum up the most important things in life. Mike and I consistently seek out messages from people and the landscape. Very often it sets the pace for our adventure. My latest fortune cookie message was "True wealth is not what you have, it's what you give." I think Isaiah slipped that one in there.

Emerson wrote an essay about giving that echoes that idea. If I remember correctly, he sings the praises of small, heartfelt gifts that are presented spontaneously to the recipient. Pointing out the folly of gift-giving as a form of currency, Emerson recommends thinking twice about both the methods and the motives of giving.

Mike and I say that giving is what we do. When we set out for the day, we hope that we are directed to say and do things that will help another person. You never know if some comment or smile will change a person's day. It could be the way you make the bank tellers laugh and feel good about themselves or it could be life-changing advice that you give a young person. Whatever it is, it undoubtedly is a gift if you remove any agenda other than a heartfelt wish to be of service to the greater good. Then, no matter what you say or do, it can't be taken wrong and there's no wondering if you *meant something* by it or expect anything in return for it. It's gift-giving, not emotional currency.

All too often we give our children gifts to express our love. When our grandparents spoke of *spoiling* children, they meant just that. When a child comes into the world, it needs to be fed and loved. That purity is spoiled right away by well-meaning parents who want to "give" their child everything, every opportunity, every lesson, every moment of protection, every possible benefit. Yet, we all know that most of those things come with some sort of agenda. We don't want them to fall behind, be teased, lack for knowledge or physical grace. But very often, our efforts backfire on us when our kids refuse to become what we want them to become. Giving so much encourages us to confuse the being and doing formulas and we forget that they are two separate things. If we could brush away all of the complexities of what we *give* our children, we might be able to simply love who they *are* and allow them to be free to explore what they need to *do* while they are here.

Don't get me wrong, just because I'm handing out this advice so freely doesn't mean that I have always followed it. I still find myself wanting to *give* my girls things. When they were little and I gave them a present they really wanted, they would tell me how much they loved me. My answer, though it sounds a little harsh, was always, "Don't love me because I got you this thing. Love me just because you do. That way, if I can't give you something you want, you'll still love me." Slowly, I think that lesson has been sinking into them. It gets harder when families split up. Too often, the expectation is amplified when one parent vies against the other with the weapon of gift-giving as a motive to win the children's affections. It's pretty common.

So where do you go when gift-giving has gotten totally out of control? I don't know. But my guess is, like any damaging habit, you have to just muster the courage to stop. Going cold turkey on the gift-giving frees you up to restore some energy, regroup, and reconsider what your true gift is.

I have seen how the giver-receiver formula changes and the receivers begin to tap into their resources and come up with something. That's when a child writes a poem or sings a song, paints a picture, or simply rushes you with hugs and kisses. If the fortune cookie message is true, why wouldn't we allow our children the wealth that giving provides? Doing so may just let them discover a gift.

In a simpler version, the kids get one good toy and a stocking filled with edible treats. At least, that's how it was when we were children. "The smell of a new doll," one of my yoga students said, "always reminds me of Christmas." A new doll. I remember what that was like. These days, children get so many new things, they develop an addiction to newness that is insatiable. There's nothing left to discover when, for instance, they can "drive" a Barbie car when they're barely old enough to walk. That's what the grandparents meant by *spoiling* a child. In our haste to give them everything we can, we take away too much.

I had a similar conversation with a veteran teacher while I was substitute teaching at the local high school last week. One of the seniors commented to her that they were the last group of children that actually liked to play outside. Most children these days would rather stay indoors where it is warm and play electronic games while they lounge on overstuffed furniture. The days of tree forts and "No Girlz Allowed!" signs are ancient history to our youth. Snowball fights, inventing ways to sled down the hill, go-carts, mud pies, and the sandlot have all been replaced by a virtual world that feeds the addiction of newness.

Where is the gift of invention in the world of the admittedly quiet and easy-to-babysit child these days? Let's face it, it is a lot easier to be able to stay connected to social media while you babysit a kid who plays candy crush while you scan your friends' profiles. Perhaps a little dose of moderation will allow for both scenarios? Nature, our first teacher, provides new things daily. It requires a little subtlety but is the ultimate game-changer. It might be a good idea for both child and babysitter to spend some time outside.

The greatest gift might be none at all. Or maybe it is just to make it simpler. Maybe it is allowing ourselves to be the recipients of some awful cookies or a handmade card. Maybe it is to slow down just a little, shut off the electronics for a day or two and take long looks. Being present might just be the best present.

HANDMADE GIFTS

My family members are used to getting stuff I have made. Sometimes this means that they get a hat that is way too small because well, they grew a lot since the last time I saw them. It can also mean that they get some really nice hand-made wool socks that they can't wear because they hate the way wool feels next to their skin.

I guess you could say that the thought was what matters – and that it's funny. Making gifts takes a little more than just loading up on *things*. It takes thought and effort. And sometimes, it takes a really good sense of humor.

If you want the gifts to be good, it takes skill. This year, most family members are getting pottery that I have made. Last year, they got coil baskets. That's because I ran out of time and it was the easiest thing to make, requiring little attention and skill. It's so easy, I can do it in the dark (something I had to do a couple of times last year!).

You can use just about any kind of string to make a coil basket but the thicker its diameter, the faster the basket will be to make. Last year I happened to acquire a big bag of assorted yarns and ribbons on the trade blanket (see Book I). One of the reels in the bag was a synthetic brown rope which made excellent coil basket material. I also cut strips of potato chip bags (I know, I shouldn't eat them…) and twisted them into foil rope. I have seen people use *plarn*, a yarn made from strips of plastic bags looped together. If you cover the *plarn* with something decorative or some interesting fabric, you can make the coils with these.

You can also use natural fibers like corn husks and green twigs. I have seen coil baskets made from long grasses like sweet grass and shorter fibers like pine needles. It's pretty cool. But, I'm not that good.

It is easiest to start with something like a piece of felt or felted wool for the base and then begin to attach the coils using a nice yarn or thread. After the first row, you'll want to create a regular pattern, either stacking the stitches up or alternating placement with each row. Your basket will grow with each row and can be shaped by either tightening or slackening the rows as you go. The last row creates a tail end that you simply tuck into the previous row. You can finish the top with a second round of loop stitches.

Handmade gifts give us an incentive to be creative and learn new skills. Sometimes being able to just go and buy gifts robs the giver of the beauty of gift-giving. It could be one of the ills of affluence. But, it doesn't have to be. It might be as simple as adding a little creativity to life. The best present under the tree might end up being some cool yarn and a crochet needle or a set of woodworking tools. Who knows? It could end up inspiring a true gift.

15. TRUE STORY
December 16, 2014

There is no such thing as a true story. Each telling and retelling is a miracle of human memory with only one goal in mind: to pass on an important message. Mike always says that some unimportant details must be sacrificed for the sake of a good story. Anyone who has ever told a story will recognize the truthfulness behind this statement.

Yet, anyone who has visited us will attest to the fact that whatever I write about here is stuff we actually practice ourselves. I couldn't have it any other way.

To both of us, integrity is key. We are not experts trying to convince other people to wake up from their world of illusion and join us in our off-grid paradise. Our objective is more about sharing thoughts and ideas that might be helpful or interesting.

How often has something really strange happened and you have thought, "You can't make this stuff up!"? *Truth is stranger than fiction.*

The way that synchronistic events have occurred to make our building easier or the house better are just too good to be true. For example, the way that Larry had some spare cabinets in his basement that came from a demolition. He was saving them for his wife but she didn't want them. Our timeline for completing the kitchen was moved up considerably because of that little piece of synchronicity. Not to mention the fact that the cabinets he gave us are much better quality than those we could have afforded, even after saving a long time.

Ever since I have been able to suspend my belief in the idea that there is such a thing as a true story, I have noticed a marked increase in the number of those types of synchronistic events happening in my life.

The truth is, ever since we let go of complete control over our lives, we have seemed to gain so much more. It seems oxymoronic (got to love that word!) that by giving up control, we actually gain more. But, that is exactly what has happened to Mike and me. Once we were able to say, "You know, this whole lifestyle is just not working for us, we need to quit it," the more we gained. The more we give away, the more we gain.

We have all heard about it. It takes a little courage and faith to put it into practice. We are just here to tell you that it really does happen. It happens without any expectation. When you least anticipate, it shows up as a surprise. Like the gift all wrapped up beautifully under a Christmas tree, it pops open in front of you and you exclaim, "Wow!! Thank you Universe! It is exactly what I needed!"

If you read *Walking Away*, you already heard about Larry, his scaffolding, and Ray with the PEX tubing. These are just examples of all of the little synchronistic events that have supplied things we have needed to build our house.

Add to that the gifts we receive from others on a constant basis, and it propels us to share what we have to give, as well. You don't give to get but getting sure makes giving feel balanced and right.

I guess you could say that giving invokes the power of attraction. What we put out to the Universe comes back to us and surrounds us. Keeping that in mind, we try to remain mindful of what we put out there and try to keep it all real.

I always love it when one person in a couple starts to tell a story and the other person corrects all of the little details during the telling of it. Before the storyteller can finish, we have lost all interest in the reason why that person told the story to begin with. You've seen this happen. It is funny, you have to admit.

When that happens to us, Mike will say flat out, "Is it important to the story?" *No? Well then why interrupt me?*

So true. I guess our stories are a little like that. I get all fussy about the details of what actually happened and in what sequence. That's why I keep journals. He is much more interested in the pertinence of the story. That's why I always read my stories to him. He helps me sort out what is important to tell.

One of my yoga students said, "Why don't you include some of the stories you tell in yoga class in your next book? They are little bits of wisdom." I really appreciated that comment on many levels. The first is that I think it's wonderful that she read my book and that she thought about it enough to think about the sequel. That kind of thoughtfulness just emphasizes what a lovely and generous person she is.

The other thing I appreciate is how important storytelling is to people, even in a simple yoga class. Setting an intention at the beginning and weaving it into the middle and the end of class makes it all flow better. The quotes I use aren't *my* bits of wisdom but I guess knowing how to keep the stories pertinent requires some.

So, how is all of this pertinent to a collection of stories about waking up from a dream world where Mike and I felt like little robots doing what is required because that's what robots do?

It is pertinent because we have been able to give up a normal way of living and carve out a new way. We have discovered that it is better than ever for us. Telling our stories provides those who wish to listen with a view of life told by those who were willing to take the risk. *It's not so bad*, they say. *It's actually pretty cool,* they reiterate. It is true.

But not every true story has to be true. One of my favorite forms of storytelling is the allegory. And one of my absolute, all-time favorite allegories is *Candide*, written by French writer, Voltaire, in the 1700's. It is interesting to me to note that Voltaire was one of the thinkers who drove the Enlightenment, the period of Western history during which our country was founded. Voltaire and his contemporaries formed the genesis of such preposterous ideas as universal human rights.

Candide is the ultimate book for anyone who is interested in thinking. Of course, since Voltaire made fun of everyone and everything in Western Europe, Asia, the New World, and Africa during his lifetime, his footnote section is longer than the story itself. That can become tedious reading unless you suspend your need for unnecessary details. The stories are unbelievable because, well, they aren't true. If you can get past wanting any technical veracity, reading *Candide* is a wonderful adventure into the world of what is true and incorruptible. Some might argue nothing, actually. I tend to disagree.

At the end of a convoluted and incredible story involving way too many characters who all have their own ideas of absolute truth, Candide realizes that the search for truth and meaning might be less important than simply "cultivating one's own garden."

He witnesses how bored and testy his group has become when after horrific lives of war and its tortures, they finally live together in comfort. The only character in the group who is happy, however, is the slave Cocombo who sings and laughs while he labors long, arduous days to provide the food and drink for the rest of the group. He plants his garden and then goes to market to trade for the luxury items his friends require to be "happy."

I think of us, especially Mike, as he makes his way to the marketplace every day, leaving before dawn to sell his labors for our prosperity. He is a happy man. We both are cultivating a cool little garden here. We are cultivating our minds and spirits. We are also cultivating a community of mind and spirit gardeners. Our stories make it so.

Blessed are the storytellers (that's all of us, I'm sure). I am eternally grateful to Voltaire for his contribution to my own sense of what is true. Since reading his allegory when I was fifteen, I learned that every person on Earth is walking around with a story to tell and is suffering in some way that is greater than anyone else is. No matter, princess who has found her prince charming, or philosopher, there is some suffering in that story that exceeds any other's suffering.

I also learned that while we all need to feel secure and prosperous, humans detest being bored. If Voltaire is correct, the best way to create someone's feeling of monotony and boredom is to provide everything for them. If that is the case, the importance of being an active participant in our own provisions (or simply put, *providing for ourselves)*, might be imperative for our feeling of happiness.

In another story of truths, Christ told his followers, "It is more difficult for a camel to pass through the eye of a needle than for a rich man to make it through the gates of Heaven." This might not necessarily mean that if you're wealthy, you'll never make it. Chances are, the parables and stories Christ told to his students have been retold a little differently (at least retold in a different language) so some tiny subtleties might have been lost in the translation. Everyone knows the difficulty of translating the connotations of meaning when retelling stories. Some of the pertinence might be lost.

The message of this little anecdotal reference might just as surely be the same one that Voltaire was getting at: *plant your garden, get out there and work to provide for your needs, simplify, and humble yourself. Whatever your standard of living, cultivate yourself, learn new things, and practice good behavior. Be grateful for small things and look for ways to help others.*

Of course, that's just my retelling of the story. It might just as easily be altogether something else.

Anyway, all good advice must be taken with a grain of salt. But, the true story seemed to allude to the bored and argumentative group of survivors in Voltaire's allegory. What they didn't seem to be able to realize is that in the long run, working out in the garden might be more important than being comfortable.

That's what I have come to realize out here. Mike and I are pretty comfortable now. That can cause a little discomfort in our relationship sometimes. The imperative needs like staving off famine and keeping warm can put things in perspective. Last year I wrote that it takes two to survive. This year I have to keep reminding myself that, more importantly, it takes two to thrive. No relationship will ever be without some grit. It is *need* that keeps two people together in spite of the grit. The truth is, both parties have to make sure it's a good thing by being a good thing in and of themselves. I feel pretty certain that being good company for yourself is the best bet. It's no guarantee, but at least when all of the dust of life settles and everybody is comfortable, being able to cultivate your own garden is what will make you happy company.

Mike and I are constantly learning how to make things better. We search for ways to make life better for ourselves and the people we know. Ultimately, though, we know that our greatest contribution to others is our integrity.

Being and doing, in our minds, comes before having. The having seems to inevitably follow when we stay true to ourselves. In our case, if I write about something, I try to make sure I attribute the source of this bit of understanding, whether it be a story, some information, or a piece of equipment that made life easier.

I guess that's what self-realization is all about. Being who you are without any apology (truth), doing what you say you're going to do (integrity), and the blessing of comfort will come. Most people reverse the order of things and end up thinking that if you have enough, you'll be able to do and be whoever you truly are. I have been thinking it could actually keep that from happening.

Maybe the real story here is simply the story of two of life's gardeners. We are focused on what we can give and how we can serve. That means we have to cultivate knowledge, skill, and energy and they must be given with heartfelt intention. Your garden must be rich in order to give from it.

True story.

PROOFING OVEN

In an effort to make things better at home for making breads, yoghurts, oil infusions, honey infusions, and anything else that requires staying between 90 degrees and 110 degrees, Mike came up with a simple plan. Living off-grid means that your house temperature can fluctuate remarkably during the day. Some days it might dip as low as 46 degrees if we are both gone. That makes it hard to keep an even temperature for proofing. Some things like oil infusions have to remain at that temperature for up to ten days.

To proof bread dough, my library friends say they just bring their oven up to temperature, turn the oven off, put their loaf in to rise, and leave it there for a little under an hour. It works nicely and I have done that. The problem with us is, it requires solar power to run our gas stove because of the glow plug. While this system works well, it just is not efficient for me.

So Mike invented a really simple solution that has opened up a whole new world of kitchen chemistry to me. He created a proofing oven out of one of the cabinets above our propane refrigerator.

By simply drilling evenly-spaced holes in the bottom of the cabinet, the proper amount of heat consistently rises from the back of the refrigerator, keeping the temperature at a continuous 93 degrees. He placed a divider between the two halves of the two-doored cabinet so I can still use the other cabinet for my cookbooks. Pretty cool. (Or should I say, *warm?)*

16. SNOW STORM
January 27, 2015

I awakened this morning with a grateful thought. It had to do with the fact that Mike and I took the time last fall to cut down the last of the trees that were too close to the house. We had cut so many trees in order to build that we were beginning to feel like it was a bloodbath. (If you've ever cut into a yellow birch, you know that trees do bleed.)

But facts are facts. When you cut trees and then stump them, it weakens all of the other nearby trees. That means that when you clear for a house, it's not just the area of the little spot the house takes up. In our case, that would only be 24'X32'.

Once the house was built, we marked the trees that might fall on the house in a bad storm. As I watch the dance of great giants as they respond to the wintery gusts of the three-day storm that is hitting us, I am glad we did.

Admittedly, the last two years have been really busy for us. Between working on our house and out in the community to pay for things, foraging, beekeeping, subbing, teaching yoga, coaching softball, hosting houseguests, writing, publishing, and promoting *Walking Away,* we have spent every ounce of energy on setting ourselves up. We often have joked that we end most of our days like two prize-fighters in their corners at the end of a match.

Today, other than just plowing, we have only two other things on the to-do list. Cook up a great steak we bought in town at the butcher's shop and watch a movie on Mike's laptop. Not bad.

Because of our work, I now have a spacious, efficient kitchen to cook in. Just before Thanksgiving, we decided to recycle some old slate roof shingles we bought in Monson for $2.00 each. I had heard that slate makes the best countertop since it is impervious to bacteria and will not burn or stain. Mike used thinset to cement the thin roof shingles to ½" cement board and then laminated that to ¾" plywood. The result is a very durable, black countertop that is almost two inches thick. The worn spots where the roof nails punctured the shingles adds interest.

When friends stop by, we sometimes say that our house is a work in progress: a lot more work than progress. Mike says you can only joke about something that isn't true. Truth is, we have made a great deal of progress, though sometimes it is hard to get things done when the house is already functional. Things on our to-do list are things that will make our house a finished house. They are things like putting up the tongue-and groove paneling that covers our tin-foil-looking insulation.

It's a lot easier to live with the tin-foil walls than to muster up the inspiration to set up all the tools, figure out scaffolding, and cover all your stuff so your sweaters don't end up coated in sawdust.

Well, that's the other thing on our to-do list we could get done this winter: a closet in our bedroom. We also could put some shelves up in the basement so our canned goods are up off the floor and the air can circulate better. Storage in the basement will help us find our tools and toys more efficiently. But, to be honest, I'm really happy that Mike put lights down there and that I have a pretty cool washing machine that saves water (which saves solar power).

Every now and again, it's important to kick back and take a look at everything you **have** done and be grateful that you had the physical and the mental capacity to do it.

Truth is, Mike has already installed lights all over the house. The kitchen, bathroom, living room, and bedrooms all have lights and outlets. I was able to run the vacuum the other day and needed to because, well, we have a nice cream-colored carpet in one of the guest bedrooms. It's not a bad place to camp out for a weekend, that's for sure.

Fortunately, Mike and I installed a slate floor throughout the house. I say that because we bought the slate at a big box store for a $1.40 a square foot. The tiles are absolutely beautiful. They are from India and range in colors between gold and deep grey with some greens and reds thrown in, as well as an occasional fossil. The only problem is that they are highly irregular and that makes installing them a bear. Mike decided to stagger them so that the irregular grout lines wouldn't be as obvious to the eye. You might laugh but that's the kind of stuff that drives my husband crazy. He hates irregular grout lines.

Of course, our bathroom shower still doesn't have **any** grout in it. That's because there are about three more tiles with special cuts that we haven't installed yet. The shower is waterproof and works just fine. That's why it's not done. Yet. It will get done. I'm not worried. I'll get around to it when I can.

That's the beauty of building together. You both have the to-do list on the house so no one stands on any moral high ground to nag the other person about getting things done. The honey-do list has two honeys doing it. Or not.

The way I see it, people are a lot more efficient when they want to do something and, well, winter just does something to you that makes you less willing to do things. To put it more gracefully, winter is for doing other things than the to-do list.

It's for lying on the couch and reading a good book (or trying to write one). It's for cooking up some baked beans, making bread, and cracking open that elderberry jam you made. It's for hugging the wood stove, curling up together with Hermes, having dinner with friends, designing tree houses, and looking outside. Personally, I love winter because it gives me an excuse to do the things I would like to be doing all year but just don't make the time to do.

Mostly, winter reminds us that it's okay just to be. We get a little fat over the holidays and winter reminds us that we don't need to be so vain. If you try to lose the few extra pounds, it's more about wanting your clothes to fit again. In the winter, no one can even tell but you if you chubbed out a little. You're still you because what you are isn't your body. It's your spirit. It's your laughter and your wit. It's your attitude and your warm smile. It's not the thing that houses all of that goodness. Winter reminds us of the truths that get lost in scantier months.

The storm continues to rage outside but we are content inside. We know there are people without electrical power right now but we have lights. We know that coastal New England is shut down for a few days, flights are cancelled, schools are closed, and some unfortunate people have had to deal with coastal flooding on top of the snow.

But today we are happy. Mike and I made ice cream with eight cups of snow, a little maple syrup, and a cup of milk. Aside from a trip or two to shovel off the deck and bring in a few handfuls of wood, our activity level is low. We aren't concerned that a tree will fall on a power line or that we won't be able to get out in the morning. Schools are closed so I won't be getting a sub call tomorrow. We will sleep soundly tonight knowing that we got the important things done.

DRIED ORANGE PEEL

If there's one thing that folks in the colder climates do have access to in the winter, it is citrus. In fact, I used to lament in Miami that if you want a good orange, you'd better plant your own tree since all of the good oranges are always sent north. (Of course, every tree that I have grown is always forcefully cut down by the citrus police who don't want you spreading an apparently deadly fungus – for citrus trees, of course. It stinks but that is a whole different story.)

Oranges in winter are such a blessing up here that, like most blessings, I like to extract as much goodness as I can from them. So here's what I do with my orange peels.

Wash them well. Place them in a fire-safe bowl on the wood stove and leave them there overnight. If you don't have a wood stove, you can use a dehydrator or radiator, or sunny windowsill. Grind when dried and save in an unoccupied spice jar with a stick of cinnamon.

I use a teaspoon of the ground powder for scones, breads, cookies, stews, stir fries, you name it. It is a very expensive item to buy if you look for it in the spice section of your grocery store. Why not make it yourself? It's easy. And it makes your house smell good.

17. FIRE
February 3, 2015

Last night Mike and I sat and watched *flamavision.* You know what it is. It is when you can't stop staring at the blazing fire in your wood stove and your brain completely melts. Your jeans get hot from the proximity but you can't stop watching. It can eat up hours of your time and you don't even notice. The only thing that gets you up is that commercial break when you have to put another log on.

It's not a bad way to relax after a hard day of whatever the cold, snowy, windy day required of you. In our case, it was replacing the carpet on the main stairway for the owner of our local grocery store. His wife was really happy with it. I think she appreciated that, in spite of the awful weather, we kept our word, and showed up. I think she was also happy with her choice of carpet and the quality installation. Our cheerful attitudes might have helped too. A lot of times our customers end up being friends. It's just how we work.

I have been thinking a lot about fire lately. From the story of Prometheus I read to students when I subbed the other day, I got to thinking about how dismal human life would still be if that Titan had not considered that humans could handle its power. He suffered an eternity of having his liver plucked out by a bird for trusting us with fire. I hope he thought it was worth it.

There are a lot of things you can use to start a fire but hurry is not one of them. In fact, nothing will make a fire putter out faster than a little hurry. It takes time to make a quick fire. It takes a slow and steady breath, little quiet puffs of air in just the right spots to keep a fire from blowing out.

Before Mike and I walked away from the ordinary circumstances our life, I had become an expert at trying to keep the little coals in my soul from burning out. For me it meant a poem on Valentine's Day or Mike's birthday. It meant writing someone a letter or jotting ideas down in my journal. Keeping the coals burning in the seat of my soul became an obsession for me that would wake me up at three o'clock in the morning and would not let me rest until I had caught the words circulating through my head and steadied them on paper.

Too many nights I would awaken with a sense of something not quite right with my world but I was too physically and emotionally exhausted to even raise my pen. Those thoughts and ideas will be gone forever. Only the ash-gray smoke of an unrecognizable memory would be left. You can't really do anything with those thoughts. They're not really ideas. Other times I would awaken with such crisp thoughts that they kindled in me an awakened state that lasted way past the alarm clock. Those were the days that I arrived late to work, star-eyed and alive with the thrill of dancing with my muse all night long.

The creative fires of a person takes its time. It truly is not something you can rush. Perhaps a full life must be lived before a person's voice is ready to be heard. And yet, there's that delicate balance between doing what needs to be done to keep up the lifestyle. Ultimately, it is important to keep the coals hot because it takes a lot more fuel to get a fire started from cold coals than it does to stoke up a fire from red-hot coals. It's worth it to get up in the middle of the night to put another log on and to log in a few words.

For most of the year up here in my new life, the two go together. There's no alarm clock timeframe telling me that my creative time is over. Like the fire, I keep it fueled when I am home, relishing the coziness of the warmth it radiates through my heart.

A day like today makes me happy as I sit in the golden glow of the fire and the blue light of my computer. The sun casts long shadows on the snow and Hermes lies at my feet. He is happiest on days like this too. I enjoy working with Mike, subbing at the school, and teaching my yoga classes, but this is my real work. I am adding kindling to the fire of my heart.

I will have to get up soon to make dinner. Mike is out at the school teaching softball players how to pitch and he'll be coming home hungry. I count on that from him. He will be really glad that I kept the fire going all day, slowly and methodically feeding the stove the wood we cut and stored a year and a half ago when we cleared our land to build. A steady approach has led me to this day when I can honor my life's purpose and write these little observations.

Our woodpile is still pretty full since we keep adding fallen trees and logs that we split last fall for use next winter. We feel an abundance that only a good wood pile can give you. Our plans this spring include building a woodshed since we built a temporary one out of the parts of the pop-up carport that collapsed last winter under the weight of way too much ice and snow.

Mike made the new structure out of the pipes and a few different tarps since the original carport cover tore apart in too many places. We knew it might not last the full season but it looks as though it might. The snow around it is about seven feet tall but, like an igloo, the snow appears to be what is holding it up. Putting our fire wood under the temporary structure was another risk but it turned out to be much better than last year's system of logs stacked on pallets and then closely covered in tarps. Like my finished lumber that I wrapped too tightly, that fire wood never got to breathe so it held on to its moisture. As a result, the wood stove never got very hot last year and built up a lot of creosote.

Since you always have to be careful with chimney fires, Mike found a way to keep the creosote level down with a powder that you scatter into a blazing fire once a week. The stove must be running pretty hot to do this. He also found these flare-type gadgets that you throw into a wood stove if it catches fire. It literally burns the fire out and saves your stove from fire-damage.

When I write that the stove burns hot, I'm talking between 300 and 500 degrees Fahrenheit on the top. That means that it also makes a good cooking surface. We made sure that since we would be burning wood for our heat, we would also use it as a stovetop and made sure we purchased one that has a lot of space on top with two levels and a wide firebox. Mike plans to make me a little cast iron oven grate that I can place in the woodstove to bake. I think he has pizza in mind with this little invention. It might be last night's dinner that got him thinking about it again.

Our friends have a Pioneer Princess wood stove that is a modern version of the old wood stoves people used in the 1800's. Our friends have decided to cook exclusively on their wood stove through the entire month of March. They have a back-up electric stove but seem to be doing just fine. We went over to their house for pizza and it was really good. It took its time cooking which allowed plenty time for their homemade chokecherry wine to warm up the conversation.

There is something about heating and cooking with wood that is noticeably different than doing so with other sources. For one thing, the log I am burning used to be a tree that I handled many times. I am not likely to take for granted something that precious to me. It cost me not only the awareness that it once was a life and supported life, but cost me a lot of effort to process so that I could eventually place it reverently into my wood stove.

There is something so attractive about fire. You know what I mean because like TV, you can't help but stare into the flames of a live fire. It always cracks me up when people have a video of a fire playing on their TV at Christmas time. But I get it. When you know how good the real thing is, you want to replicate it, even though it's nowhere near the real thing. It's just another parallel universe thing.

One of our last full memories of our house in Rhode Island is when the police and fire department (with full fire truck) showed up when my husband and I had not pulled a permit for a backyard fire one night. The rule is that you have to get a permit to make a fire. The permit is only good for that day and expires at eleven o'clock at night. It kind of takes the spontaneity out of life when you have to visit the police station before you decide to sit around a fire after work to stare at the fire and listen to its stories with your neighbors.

Our friends love hanging out around the fire up here. We gather plenty of "squaw wood" (that's the dry, low lying branches on a pine tree) for kindling and challenge each other to make a fire without matches. It's a lot of fun to watch someone make a fire for the first time.

Mike is home now and he has placed the stool in front of the fire. He is watching *flamavision* again tonight. For some reason, he doesn't tire of the stories the fire tells.

MAKING A FIRE

Fire is a tough guy. It likes to be poked at and shoved around but never smothered. It needs slow and steady attention. It will lose all interest in you if you give it too much too soon but if you walk away from a fire too soon, it will grow cold and gray. Once you get a good fire going, its coals will burn all night and will be easy to start up again in the morning without much effort.

Bet you thought you were reading *50 Shades of Hay* for a moment, didn't you?

Now, these things are all true. I have been struggling with creating the best system to make a fire for a couple of years now. One thing I found is that it's not a spectator's sport. The hardest way to start a fire is to try and show somehow how you do it. It's not something that you can rush or do half-heartedly. You must focus your attention on the fire. I think that's why men are usually in charge of getting the fire going. Women are usually in charge of several things simultaneously (try to make dinner by doing only one thing in a focused manner – you'll have a one-item meal). Okay, I'm generalizing, but you get what I mean.

So, focus is number one. Get ready to do only one thing. If you do, you'll be able to get to the other things sooner anyway. The next thing you have to do is get your kindling in order. If you are starting a fresh campfire, make a little nest of dried things like white birch bark, leaves, and small twigs. A really good fire-starter for hiking or kayaking is cotton balls soaked in Vaseline (you warm up the Vaseline and then soak the cotton balls). White birch bark is excellent kindling and will ignite even when damp. Make tiny strips of the bark and rub them in your hands to release the bark's oils. Starting with tiny bundles that would fit in the palm of your hand first is wise, then matchstick sized, and so on. Organizing your kindling in increasingly large bundles beforehand is very helpful. Using smaller diameter branches like the lower branches sticking out of pine trees is really good.

For us, getting a spark isn't the hard part. We use a striker rod with magnesium to get ours going. You don't have to keep it dry and you use the dull part of your knife to cut into the rod which forms a spark. You scrape off a little magnesium and gather it into your fire nest to catch the spark which easily ignites. If you watch survivor shows, they will inevitably do this part wrong. Remember to go SLOWLY when it comes to fire. On TV, they try to do it like you would strike a match.

If you're ever on a survivor show or you are really in survival mode because you got lost in the woods, you can make a bow drill out of a stick and some chord. But that is something you have to learn to do in person and I couldn't teach you. I did it once. I'm not sure I could do it again. It requires A LOT of perseverance. Since I know how hard it is to start a fire this way, I try to keep a fire rod on me whenever I go out, just in case.

At home we use a propane torch. That's not a quaint little picture but it sure is practical. Again, the hard part is keeping the flame going, not getting it started.

When you do get the fire going, make sure you slowly add dry wood in larger increments before you put a *shitton* (a unit of measure I never knew until I moved to Maine) of wood on top. (That's the smothering part.) Arrange the smaller wood in a crisscross manner or a teepee so that air can get in. Fire needs to breathe. It needs to be fed in slow increments, not crammed full of stuff.

Once you've got a good commitment going from the fire itself and you can hear the crackles and groans of the wood burning, you know that it is time to put on the bigger wood. Okay, that will be enough of that.

18. FRIENDS
March 9, 2015

When you embark on such a fool's mission as we did, to carve out a spot in the woods where there is no electricity and no running water, you find out which of your friends is a little crazy too. They're the ones who will show up and give you some cool water to drink, a few words of encouragement, or days of looking at plans and lifting logs into place.

It was the second weekend in November, 2013. I will never forget the tears in Quimbly's, eyes as she took one last look before driving away. My incredibly good and able friend was worried. I was too. Mike was too but he couldn't show it. I think his own tears were just frozen to his face as he was attempting to shingle the roof between snow storms. He was hoping for a break in the weather so that he could finish the roof. (That break never happened and when temperatures dropped to 19 degrees, he finally gave up trying to get it done.) The snow came early that year and, though the very last thing Quimbly helped Mike do was to cut a hole in our roof for the wood stove chimney, parts of our roof were nothing but tar-papered.

Winter had caught us in the middle of everything and it hit hard. It was hard for her to leave knowing that we would be a little more vulnerable than we had planned but what else could she do? She had a job and a normal life to get back to.

But Quimbly and others had been there for the times when we really needed it most. Friends gathered for work parties and helped us screw planks on our decking, build up our walls, seal up the cracks between logs, and generally just lighten the load. For one friend who couldn't make it, her sweatshirt was enough.

"Patty told me not to let anyone wear her sweatshirt. She doesn't want it to get ruined in the construction." That was Quimbly's way of egging us on to ALL wear the sweatshirt. Everyone who showed up that work weekend wore Patty's sweatshirt and we sent her pictures. There were at least thirty pictures, including a horse wearing the sweatshirt. The last picture was of Quimbly washing the sweatshirt in the river. *Thanks for the good time, Patty.*

I know the etymology of the word friendship doesn't include the idea that it is a ship that can take you immediately away from a boring or tense situation while no one around you notices. Come on, think of it: you're in that meeting and the presenter is droning on and on about stuff you really aren't that interested in but you're hoping to get that promotion so you have to look interested and then, all of a sudden you remember the time you and your friend were stuck in traffic on the highway and you had to pee so badly that you got out and tried to hide behind the car door and your friend closed it on you as a joke.

You want to smile but your presenter might notice. So you do your best to hold it back. Then you think about that sunset you both shared on the beach and your mind skips to the time you both jumped in the ocean on New Year's Day as a fundraiser and you lost your flip-flops and had to run out barefoot in the snow.

Actually, the etymology of the ship in friendship has more to do with the Old English word for create or to make. When we get together with friends, it brings out every good thing in us: laughter, love, creativity, activity, adventure, and sometimes those tears we can't bear to let free in anyone else's company.

If there's one thing Mike and I have in common, it's that we consider each other good friends and relate as friends most of the time. We also love each other's friends, no matter what, because having them around gives us a chance to play.

Having fun with our friends is a priority. Though being up here in the woods has made us a little more isolated, it has given us more time for play. As a result, we get to play with our friends more than we ever did before. They know that we'll have something crazy and fun up our sleeves, even if we planned to do nothing. Sometimes all it takes is to make an apple pie in the campfire with Grandma's cast iron pan to make us all happy. Give everyone a soup spoon and no plate and you've got an unforgettable experience.

Even the annoying things are fun with friends. The best toys are those little tennis racket bug zappers during black fly season. My girlfriend and Mike created a world-class light show for us the summer we broke the foundation. The sound effects were something to behold as they danced around together with their little rackets. If you don't have one, it's worth it to get one and go out in a mosquito bog just to feel the power.

There's no doubt that when we play, we open ourselves up to healing laughter and a joy for living. Friends remind us that no matter how irritating we can be, we are nonetheless lovable. We might get the eye roll or be called things we might not want to mention, but it's always to our face and we can't help but laugh when it happens or laugh when we think about it.

Friendship asks for nothing but won't last unless both parties are givers. Our friends are the ones that will tell us we have a booger in our nose or say, "hey, was that you who just gassed us?" They aren't going to offend you even if you were offensive. It's just that way.

And then, there's the creativity of play that our friends help us manifest. The more Mike and I play, the better we get at returning to our responsibilities with a relaxed mind, renewed energy, and a more creative approach to our problems.

Of course our friends work with us too. And, we gather friends from unlikely sources, like contractors we work for, our bosses, and our customers. Being able to collect friends is an art. Emerson once said that in order to have a friend, you must first be a friend. I like that. Mike has taught me that friendship doesn't have to be this heavy box of photographs. You don't need to hold on to every shot taken of two people and every birthday card ever given. To him, friendship is light and easy. He never remembers birthdays, doesn't want to see pictures of people's grandchildren or cats and he'll tell them so. He might make fun of someone's size and give that person a nickname that sticks forever to show how much he loves him.

He reaches out to old ladies, wrinkled veterans, children, and very shy types. He doesn't do that, "well, maybe they want to be left alone" thing. He assumes everyone could use a little laughter, a little attention, and a little playfulness in their day. He lives with the idea that no matter how serious things get, there is always time for a little jocularity. He never hesitates to reach out to someone in friendship. It's just the way he is.

Spending so much time with your spouse and trying to accomplish tough things with that person isn't always roses and laughter. People get into moods (I'm not going to say which one of us) and it's important to be able to remember that we are all just a collection of molecules with mostly space in between so moods and unintended bad attitudes can just pass right through us if we don't give them a purchase in our hearts. I guess that's what forgiveness teaches us.

When the hurts just keep coming with no regard for our feelings at all, that's abuse and we need to speak up and, depending on the intensity, get out. When it is tiredness talking, it is best to just let it go and expect the same when the tables turn. We gain everything by giving a little. Friendship teaches us to be resilient and laugh at our own foibles.

We have learned about our edible landscape from our friends. In fact, just about everything we have learned how to do, we have either learned from a friend or taught ourselves and then taught a friend.

When our friend C. came to visit, she taught us about animal tracks, tree identification in the winter, and how to make a living room in the snow with open sky as its ceiling. This has given us the opportunity to invite other friends over for a campfire even though we have five feet of snow on the ground. To make it comfortable, we dug little sofa shelves in the wall around the fire pit and lined them with balsam branches. Our friends know to bring their ski pants when they come over for dinner.

If there's one thing I have noticed about the friends we have made up here, it is this simple truth. Most have come here to reconnect and simplify. There's a certain integrity to this kind of attraction to a place. Obviously, we are all interpreting that concept our own ways. While some friends want to teach us about the ways and means of pig farming, others are teaching us about finding fiddlehead ferns along the river banks.

Any way I look at it, when my friends get together, there is an excitement in the air that can only be caused by the power of a brain that is high on learning and creating. Taking a creative leap of faith like building a house off-grid in the middle of the woods is a lot easier when you've got friends helping, even when, eventually, they will have to leave you alone with your own tomfoolery.

BERRIES

Apart from the annoyingly loud buzzing noises of chain saws and the murderous pace of the logging trucks that barrel down our dirt roads, I have come to truly appreciate the logging industry. This is mainly because the bare tracks of land they leave behind do not stay bare for any length of time and the new growth is delightful to many plants, animals, and humans.

For one thing, berry plants love the clean slate that clear-cutting affords. When the larger plants are cut, the shorter plants get sunlight and don't have to compete as hard to root and produce. I guess it's unnecessary to state that the animals all benefit from the berries, even the two-legged kind. Workers in the logging industry come in, take what they need and then move on so there is little or no human traffic on those back roads. Except, of course, for a couple of weeks in the summer when a few two-leggeds find their way to the back roads and harvest a berry patch here and there.

Berry picking is a lot more fun when you go with friends. It is a lot like text messaging, only you end up with baskets of fruit at the end, something to smile about later, and a little suntan on your shoulders.

 Because you're talking to someone from behind a bush, conversations go a lot like this, "I think I'm going to bake a bread when I get home."

"What'd you say, you found something dead over there?"

Berry picking with friends is also safer because the bears and other critters hear you talking and won't get startled inadvertently. Up here our seasons go from strawberry (the wild ones are really tasty but tiny so we usually go to a farm and pay by the quart basket), wild raspberry (also small but worth the three hours it takes to fill up a quart or two), blueberry (similar experience only on your knees the whole time), and blackberry (now you're filling up fast), elderberry (getting the tiny berries off their stem takes time when you get home), and then autumn olive (extremely bountiful!).

Raspberries have soft little rasps on their stems that can leave little scratch marks on your arms. That's no big deal because in early spring you need to wear sleeves anyway. It is chilly in the morning. Blackberries are an altogether different story. It's usually hot when we pick them but you have to wear a substantial long sleeved shirt, jeans, and boots. Blackberry brambles are tough but if you're careful, you can harvest their fruit without a scratch. They will, however, grab your shirtsleeve with a tenacity that most other plants seem to lack.

If you're moving a little too carelessly for their taste, Blackberry brambles let you know with that kind of, "hey, not so fast, buster!" grab of your arm. Every now and again they like to remind you to be grateful when you harvest their fruit. "There's more than enough," they seem to say. "Stop acting like it's a race. And you had better process these guys right away because I won't tolerate you wasting my fruit!"

I think of them as the Grandmother berries because of the message I get from them. I think that's why they are my favorite. I also like the seeds and leave them in my jams and fruit leathers. Most recipes call for sifting out half of the blackberry seeds. Berry seeds are really good for the body, serving as little scrub brushes in the digestive tract and making their phytonutrients more absorbable. That's why I leave them in.

Since our freezer space is limited, I use the following methods to preserve berries.

I make fruit leathers to put in our muesli and breads by either processing them in a blender, cooking them with a little brown sugar, or squeezing them through a food mill.

Your methods will all depend on what berries you gather and how many you have. This is a good method.

Some berries are good to dehydrate directly. If you use blackberries, I recommend that you parboil them to break open the little juicy sections. They are tough and make dehydrating virtually impossible. Raspberries dry up rapidly but end up a bit small. Blueberries are the same but pack a punch in scones and breads.

I also like to use a good cider vinegar like Dr. Bragg's (eventually we will make our own cider vinegar) to make berry-infused vinegars for our salads and for cooking. Just let the berries steep in the vinegar for at least ten days. Then strain. They are really pretty with a sprig of rosemary or thyme in the bottle and can make nice gifts. This method preserves the phytonutrients of the berries and tastes delicious.

As I mentioned in *Walking Away*, I make cordials with berries but I have a backlog of cordials so I have slowed down with these.

I also do freeze some berries in small baggies for our fruit smoothies. Our friends like the potent fruit in their smoothies when they visit. We like feeding them well while they are here. It is a win-win.

19. ENOUGH
March 28, 2015

When he saw the zip-lock bag full of quarters we put on the counter, our mechanic's face cracked in half. We had just plunked down a hundred dollars in singles and fives on top of the twenties and hundreds that we had saved up to pay for our car to be fixed.

Ricky waved his tough, oil-stained hand in a motion to suggest we forget the bag full of change.

"Oh, no," Mike said, "We counted every quarter to make sure we pay you. You're gonna have to take it."

Ricky acquiesced. It's hard to be serious about such a funny thing. Our car repair had cleared us out, even down to our spare change, but we were delighted that we were able to do it. It's how we do things.

Our car, named after the Sherman Tank because it would do whatever we asked of it (including riding up a river bed with two kayaks on top when we got lost once), finally spilled its guts on our icy road last year after our plow truck burned to the ground. Sherman sat (Maine-style) in our yard for almost a year before we hired Ricky to get it back on the road. Mike knew that what was torn off old Sherman would not be an easy fix, even for him. He knew it would be a pricey one too.

Ricky was fair. It took him a lot of time to find the part and install it. It was well worth the money and, even though the amount turned out to be more than we had planned, we were happy to pay it. Starting again from zero is not new to us.

I'm not going to be so foolish as to claim that being broke has no effect on us. I can always tell when Mike is worried about making ends meet when he has those toss-and-turn nights. I get a little short of patience and tend to get negative about things. This is true.

Nevertheless, we know to remind each other that we always seem to have enough. We have an indomitable faith that if we dedicate ourselves to service, whatever that means and wherever that leads, we will be able to pay for or acquire what we need happily.

Having just enough makes us aware of those compulsive buys that seem to only satisfy for a moment and then are regrets. There's no room for those kinds of purchases. Though we can do without more easily, we both have more than we need in the way of personal items and other comforts. We certainly are not lacking.

Truthfully, by having just enough, we have gained quite a bit in the way of patience, discrimination, and efficiency. When we look for clothes now, we think fabric and use. For Mike that means thin, microfiber sweatshirts that dry fast and don't stain easily. We both like them better than the bulky cotton sweatshirts that he used to wear. If we see wool on a reduced or consignment rack, we usually find a way to buy it. We save money for good coveralls but our jeans are usually from the discount stores.

For me, it means being a little more creative with my clothes, sometimes refashioning things that are inexpensive so that they'll work for me. As a sub in a high school, I must be clean and look presentable, but it's okay if I wear the same jacket every day. I just change up the scarf and my hair style. Having longer hair is easier in that way. It doesn't require a great stylist or a blow dryer. My hair is better a little uncombed anyway. It's just the way I roll.

Having just enough is quite luxurious, if you think about it. I used to spend way too much on my hair and hair products to not stand out. Now I don't mind standing alone in my style and going gray is an interesting experiment. My grandmother did it all by herself. She didn't need a stylist's permission or instructions. And it makes me question at what point does a person stop trying to look young when they're not so.

I have always thought that it's never the dress, it's the girl in it that is beautiful. A happy, healthy girl can look good in anything you put on her, especially if she wears a genuine smile. Being fit and happy with yourself is much more important than what you wear. It saves money since most of the time, we spend money when we have to buy new clothes that fit better. I have my weight range of plus or minus five pounds and I try to keep within that range. In the long run, it helps me keep my health expenses lower if I do that. Maintaining my weight might be for vain reasons but it's also for sane reasons.

I used to spend $60.00 a month on a family membership to the gym. That was a good deal because I was a teacher at the local high school. Now, I'm getting paid to share my passion for yoga with members of my town. I am more disciplined with my yoga now. The days when I might have gotten lazy and missed class don't exist for me anymore. I *have* to show up.

I also used to buy $5.00 loaves of bread that didn't seem to fill us. Making my own bread makes sense and saves cents (really dollars when you add it all up). Now I can spend $15.00 at the grocery store on fresh vegetables and maybe a little butter and create whole food dinners for the week. One slice of Family Loaf feeds and fills. Having enough encourages simplicity and thoughtfulness.

The more Mike and I are content with enough, the wealthier we feel. And, incidentally, the more work tends to come our way. The less we concern ourselves with *having* things, more trades and gifts find their way into our hands. It appears that the Universe and its helpful agents are pleased with our faith that if we do what is right for us and use our energy to serve, we will always have enough.

When I apply that same reasoning to foraging, I know I'm doing it right. Michael Douglas from Maine Primitive School wrote recently that foraging is completely unsustainable when we approach it with the mindset of consumerism. When we approach nature as consumers, we lose the conscious thought that we take only what we need. We become what some Native American peoples called *wasichus*, the insatiable ones.

The rule of thirds teaches us that we only take 1/3 when we harvest so the plant can regenerate and propagate. It also guarantees that if you visit the same spot after someone has already been there, you'll find something and leave something.

It seems to boil down to the idea that if we can remember to have faith that we will always have enough and we remind ourselves to be grateful for the fact that we do always seem to have enough, we always will. It sounds complicated, but it's really pretty simple.

Enough is a feast.

TREE TEAS

Mike and I were recently invited to attend a Micmac pow-wow. They call it a *Maiomi*, a meeting of peoples. While there, I was intrigued by a woman in a little tent who had nine big blue water jugs set out on a table in front of her. Without entering the immediate area, you couldn't see who was manning the tent because of the tall blue stack of jugs. Tucked behind the table was Bobby Two-Feathers who sits in a wheel chair.

People of all ages crowd around her table all day long, waiting for a chance to sample the teas in her blue jugs: her *tree teas*. Each one, she tells me later, came to her in a vision. There may be more, she tells me. She takes her time and waits to see what is next but shares what she has been given in the meantime.

As we sample each tea, she asks us to relate where in the body we are feeling the tea. It is a subtle shift. For one tea, it may be in the heart, back of the throat, or top of the head. For another, it could be a general warming.

"This one here is white pine. Twenty times more vitamin c than orange juice," Bobby Two-Feathers said.

Then there's the cedar tea: a wonderful cleanser for the entire body.

"Chaga is used for its ability to cure certain diseases like diabetes and cancer."

I had heard about chaga. In fact, Mike found a large chunk of it on one of the white birch trees on our property a few years back and we have been drinking it ever since. I drink it whenever I am sick to boost my immune system. There is no question that chaga is powerful. I drank a steady stream of it while I recovered from the spider bite. I know it helped me recover so rapidly.

When a friend of ours had reached his limit with the pain he was experiencing in his kidneys, he happened to be visiting us. He asked if I knew about anything that would help. I knew about goldenrod but something was telling me to google chaga and its benefits. The information seemed to resonate with our friend so he asked if he could have some. We packaged up a little ground chaga for him so he could use it right away and Mike told him to put a few tablespoons in the bottom of an old coffee pot and leave it on the woodstove.

"Just keep adding water until it no longer comes out tea color, then add a tablespoon more of the chaga. At some point, in about a month, clean it all out and start again," Mike explained.

I guess our friend must have felt the effects promptly because a few weeks later he called to say thank you.

"My asthma, something I have had since I was a kid, is under control for the first time in my life. I can't believe how good I feel. I'm going to need more," he said. That's when Mike showed him how to find chaga growing on the side of white and yellow birch trees.

It looks like a burl or a part of the bark that was charred. If you remove it, there is a reddish brown interior and it is woody in texture. Be sure that what you remove from a birch is chaga, though. Mike and I have seen a lot of misinformed people selling chaga on the internet and it IS NOT chaga. Also, don't use tea bags for your chaga. Allow the chaga to steep directly in water. It should look and taste a lot like black tea.

A lot of us who use chaga have noticed that when people hear about a beneficial wild plant and it becomes the "Plant *du jour*," people have a tendency to overharvest. This is due to the fact that you can make money on selling it on the internet, taking a consumerist's approach to nature's bounty. This is exploitation, not implementation. Being mindful is key.

20. PAPERWORK
March 28, 2015

The letter from the State of Maine demanded that I call immediately. I hadn't checked my mail for over a week so I was already late. Not being a person who likes to deal with paperwork and numbers, I had put it off for another week before I called.

The letter said that I needed to send in copies of my Federal taxes and a letter from my town indicating what my taxes were for the previous year. The State of Maine wanted to know why my earnings were less than my property taxes last year.

My reaction to the question was completely irrational. Because I hate paperwork so much, I am manic about getting my taxes done. I don't want to have to think about them again. That's why I couldn't bear getting that letter. *I had already filed my taxes, what more do they want from me?*

My fear was that the State of Maine wanted to charge me taxes on the retirement fund I cashed in from my job in

Rhode Island. My accountant had warned me this might happen. I had already paid those taxes two years ago (a pretty hefty chunk of it too). But *maybe*, I reasoned, *they think I should pay Maine taxes on it too?*

When Mike and I set out on our journey of a self-reliant lifestyle two years ago, we weren't completely convinced that everything we had undreamed would just go away. Our plan was to scale down enough so that eventually our tax bill would be the only fixed bill we received in the mail. We knew we would have some residual income tax to pay on using the lump sum but did our best to pay them up front. I would be happy to give up paperwork, even if I had to use an outhouse for a year to make it happen. I just wanted all of that stressful paperwork to disappear.

But it didn't.

"Ma'am, I'm just pointing out that things don't add up. How could you pay your property taxes when you made so little?" The woman was being patient.

"That's the point, I can't yet but I will; I always do. Listen, I don't want anything from the government. I just want to be left alone."

"Well Ma'am, you must be making money somehow. How have you been living?"

I got nervous that she might think me a scofflaw. Living an "alternative" lifestyle sometimes makes you feel a little defensive. I mean, I'm sure there must be *something* wrong with trading and foraging. It's not something the government can tax. (Yet.)

What if everyone did that? We wouldn't have schools and roads and police, right? (This is the stuff that goes on in my head while I'm listening to all of the forms I now need to submit to The State of Maine.) I'm getting anxious and my number dyslexia kicks in and I can't remember what year I cashed in my retirement, when I moved to Maine, or even my birthday. I can't breathe and I'm struggling with a muddle of numbers in my head.

"Well Ma'am, since I can't get the information I need from you, you're going to have to mail me a copy of your Federal Income Tax for last year. We have to review your Maine 1040; fill out Worksheet B; Schedule NR, and Worksheet A; we need to review your PTFC to make sure you're a Maine resident; and you'll need to submit a 1099 showing that your retirement was your income when you lived in Rhode Island and you paid your taxes on that."

My head was spinning and I felt sucked back into the vortex of endless paperwork. I was lining up all of the justifications for why I decided I want to simplify. My notes from the conversation were beginning to look like a spoon full of alphabet soup.

I began identifying with the simple fellow in *Plato's Cave* who got to escape. I was at the part when he went back into the darkness to tell his cave-mates, *"Hey guys, you wouldn't believe how beautiful and bright it is out there! There are trees and birds, and butterflies and man, you should see the dragonflies in the sunlight!*

This puppet show you're watching (replace puppet show with the word **screen** *for emphasis here), it's not real, guys! Trust me."*

If you know the story, you'll remember that the guy's cave-mates get annoyed with him for insisting that HIS reality was the right one. That is why they pummel him to death. It never matters that your reality might be a better one. If it doesn't fit the norm, it is useless to normal people.

Plato knew that there is something about the normalcy of the cave, and our fear of what would happen if we leave, that makes us want to stay there. This whole paperwork issue was making me feel sorry I ever left my work-a-day cave where my taxes were all taken out of each paycheck and I got money back at the end of the year. This new place was beginning to scare me.

There was no way this lady sitting in a little office somewhere in a Portland high rise would understand why anyone would choose to trade in a three-bathroom house for an outhouse in the middle of the woods because of an aversion to *paperwork.*

By the end of our conversation, my tax lady had lost her patience.

"Ma'am, you have told me your whole life story but have given me nothing I can use to get this form completed. Just send in what I asked for. Thank you. Have a nice day."

It took me well into the next day to shake off my anxiety from that taxing phone call. But when I finally calmed down enough to analyze the situation and discuss it with Mike, I realized that all the lady wanted to know is how to correctly fill out the State of Maine Property Tax Fairness Credit that helps people pay their property tax when they don't make enough to do so.

I realize that my conviction to not depend on the government for anything is a bit of false pride here since the property tax program is designed to give money back to the towns that the state has been absorbing.

I think I'd better call that lady back. Maybe I can get away with filing only part of that daunting list of acronyms to get my tax credit. Maybe she does understand why I have an outhouse. Maybe she has one too.

Maybe the best approach to paperwork is to open those envelopes when they arrive in the mail. I need to simply face my fears, make the phone calls, and fill out every bit of paperwork they ask for in a timely manner.

SKIP BREATHING AND SLEEPY TEA

When life gets my mind all riled up and I can't sleep, I find that it can last for a few days, maybe even a week. I use a type of breathing that is called "skip breathing" to quiet my mind and regulate my breath. The cycle of breaths is easy to remember and I learned to do it in my yoga teacher training.

You breathe in for five counts, hold it for five counts, and exhale for five counts. It is that simple and is quite effective.

Another thing I do is I mix up a soothing tea of ingredients I collect myself. If you don't live in the Northeast, you can purchase these flowers or you can research which herbs in your area contribute to a calm mind.

Another thing to remember is that flowers like St. John's Wort shouldn't be taken by people who are on medications (especially antidepressants). We also use the flowers of valerian which can be a strong sleep aid. You can purchase valerian root tincture or gel caps (they taste like dirty socks), and chamomile. All of these herbs are not recommended if you are in your first trimester of pregnancy.

Another flower we use is lavender but some other herbs can be safely used as well, including basil for calming.

21. SPLITTING UP
June 28, 2014

When we moved our four hives from Rhode Island last February (I know, but it was the only time we could), we created a makeshift bee yard on our deck with some of the scaffolding Larry lent us. We wrapped them up in tar paper, packed them with some high protein patties we made, and let nature take its course. Our bees just needed to bundle up, conserve energy, and eat well - pretty much the same thing we were doing all winter. There's a parallel universe when it comes to understanding your bees. As in human life, stopping to listen is more important than rushing to tell.

By the spring, we were left with two strong hives and one very weak hive. We lost the hive most exposed to the wind. We also were left with a wooden deck full of bee poop. It's one of those funny things in life. I mean, how much can a bee really poop? Right. Well, consider that we had about

80,000 bees on our deck (our brand new cedar deck) all making cleansing flights on sunny winter days and you get the picture. Cleaning up after my little buzzing house pets, I concede, was worth every bit of effort just to see them alive and well at the end of a tough winter. A little scrubber and some sandpaper has made everything right again.

The problem we encountered was that moving the bees all the way from Rhode Island on a little utility trailer by myself in the middle of February proved to be much easier than moving them off the deck and into our garden. We have spent most of the spring clearing and building their new home. That meant researching the best electric fence to keep bears and other critters out. We know for sure we have a bear in the area. It might seem cruel but Mike and I would much rather zap her with a little electricity than with our Winchester. The fence has its own little solar array and a marine battery and it works just fine. It also keeps Hermes from rolling around in my freshly planted garden beds.

So, when we had our bee meeting two weeks ago, we decided that we would start with Hive Number One, the apparently strongest hive. We would open it up, check the honey supply, check the brood, and locate the queen. If there's brood, there's a queen. Unless, of course, you happen to squish her by accident when you open the hive. It's unlikely but always something to consider.

The first thing we noticed with Hive One is that it was alarmingly lightweight. These bees had no honey! To top it off, they had lots of mouths to feed and just as many on the way. It was time to take off the empty honey boxes and get some feed ready for them. They will need the calories to get them by until they can locate a source of nectar. Checking for the queen, we scanned all of the frames of brood.

In my inimitable way, I scanned each frame, searching for the type of energy that the worker bees exhibit when they are protecting their queen. It is a subtle enterprise and must be done carefully. I was taking my time. We were both in full bee suits and had the smoker going with white birch and cedar burning. This aromatic attar is a soothing tonic for us humans but is a cause of distress for the bees since it mocks a forest fire which causes them to return to the hive to feed up in case they have to move. You can see the problem here since our bees had no feed. They were getting surly and so was Mike because I was apparently taking too long in my search for the queen.

"We'd better get these guys buttoned up." Mike's voice filtered through the bee suit was more muffled than usual. "Come on, you know she's in there and she's laying. Let's get going."

I am thinking, *these guys are really gals, by the way, and I really want to see the queen. I don't know. It's just one of those girl things I guess, like wanting to see pictures of the British Royal wedding. I just want to see what she looks like.* But, I agree.

We put the hive back together while I droned on about not being able to find the queen. Mike said he was going inside for a minute and I told him that he had been walking around with a cluster of bees topping his bonnet all morning.

We don't need bees in the house, especially not angry bees. Using the bee brush to shoo them off by the front of the hive, I immediately noted that our Queen Bee had been lording it over our antics on top of Mike's head since we opened the hive. Our scaffolding bee yard had created a mini obstacle course that required Mike to pass the hive boxes over the cross bars and, consequently, over his head.

I gently lifted our queen off of his bonnet and placed her onto the landing where she preened for a minute and then regally marched right back into her hive with her entourage in tow. (Great sigh of relief here.)

Hive Number One was all checked off and ready to go. I made their feed more sugar than water so they wouldn't have to work hard to dehydrate it and added my usual lemongrass and spearmint essential oils which keeps the tracheal mites out of their systems and pretty much guarantees they'll find the feed and will use it.

We decided we needed to move the hive before adding the top feeder. The hive was light but stacked tall. Keeping the bees in the hive so that we could move it proved more of an issue since they were outside both day and night trying to find food. It took several days of waking up at 4:30 or 5:00 to check to see if they were back in their boxes to finally just say, *we're doing it and hope we don't lose too many bees in the process.*

When you move a hive, you have to make sure they're all inside, and you must give them a day to settle down. Then, when you relocate them, you have to place a leafy branch by the opening so they sense it is a new location and they reset their little GPS's. That way, when they leave the hive to forage, they can find it again.

Good communication is imperative when dealing with bees. That means listening more than speaking. They will tell you what bothers them. When we close up their hives after an inspection, it sometimes takes the lives of a couple of bees. When a bee dies, you will sense a change in the bees' tone. A bee will release a particular pheromone when it dies unnaturally. This is the defense mechanism that alerts the colony to be on guard as someone or something has infiltrated and it's not pretty. That's why you try not to rush into anything when it comes to the bees. Slow and even movements cause less casualties.

Keeping a hive open too long can get them upset too. The shift in their world order leaves them feeling exposed. This is especially true when the bees need food. If you stop to think about it, they are just like us. They just want to communicate their needs. If you've ever gotten a bee in your bonnet, you know they WILL be heard, even if they have to sting you. It kills them to do it. (It will, eventually, because they get caught in your hair and you freak out trying to get them out, and they freak out because they are trapped in your tangled mass.) It hurts you both when you panic but you can't help it and neither can they. For us, this panic results in a bee sting; for the bee, it results in death.

When we opened Hive Number Two, we immediately could tell that they had found the nectar flow. They had a good supply of honey and the colony was replete with brood. Good signs. It took us three days to move the hive, though. The bees kept bearding up on the outside and would not go back in. It wasn't because they lacked food. It had to be another reason. We had to get them all back in the hive to move them off the deck and into the garden.

At about 4:30 a.m. on the third day, Mike blocked the hive entrance and any escape routes, pretty sure he had all of the bees inside. For about three weeks, I had been waking him up before sunrise every morning, and both he and the bees were getting testy.

When we finally moved Hive Two to the garden, we were sure our days of 4:30 wake up calls were over. *Not so fast.* Half of the hive found a way to escape and decided to show up on the porch, confused about where their colony went. This required Mike to call an emergency bee meeting.

"The way I see it, we have three options: a) try to capture these bees and reintroduce them to their hive's new location," Mike was obviously concerned that we were in over our heads at this point, "b) give them a new box to settle into and see if we can find them some brood and honey and hope they have time to raise their own queen, or c) try to buy a queen and hope it gets here in time to save the hive."

I thought for a long moment. "It seems that with the bees, we have to go with their nature, taking the Taoist approach, rather than try and fight it. I don't think option A is even a real option."

"Yes, you're probably right. Let's go back into Hive Two and see if we can take some honey and brood; trying to find the youngest brood so they can raise their own queen."

We took our time, making sure that we didn't take the queen back to the new hive, which would have really made a mess of things. What we found, besides some really riled up occupants, was two queen cells that had just hatched within the last day. The reason why the bees were bearding up is that the hive was creating new queens in anticipation of a swarm.

Nature had already solved our queen problem. And we had caught it just in time to get the swarm in a hive box that we could manage. We quickly transported the frame with the new queen back to the box on the porch along with frames of unhatched brood and frames of honey. We said our prayers to the great Queen Bee in the sky and it looks like we have a split! The bees helped us get it done.

We just had to stop, take our time, and listen to what they were trying to tell us. This gave us two strong hives and two happy beekeepers. The only problem now is, we have to move Hive Number Four, but that shouldn't be a problem once they settle down.

HONEY

On first glance, all honey appears to be the same, but it is not. There is a reason why people are beginning to search farmer's markets for local honey or consider keeping bees themselves.

We have all heard (well, I assume that we all have heard) that local honey is good for allergies because it contains the pollen of local plants and helps build our immunities to the dusty culprits. However, there are other much more important reasons to seek out a local beekeeper than relief from allergies.

For one, much of the honey you buy in larger markets is produced in China. If you pay attention, almost all honey you see in stores is the exact same color. When you check out local honey (even from the same beekeepers) the honey will appear in different shades, depending on the year and what was in bloom at the time.

The monochromatic stuff that is pumped out of factory apiaries is bee-processed corn syrup and sugar water. Certain labs have discovered no pollen in mass-produced and pasteurized honey. It's a waste of money and isn't any better for you than it is for the bees.

What you want to spend your money on is raw honey. It is filtered but not pasteurized. Once you pasteurize honey, it loses its natural enzymes. Other than the pollen content, the live enzymes are what is so beneficial about honey.

Honey, real honey, is the only edible substance that will not spoil. It contains natural antibacterial and antiviral qualities. It has been reported that honey was found in the Egyptian tombs and is still as fresh as the day it was extracted from the hive, thousands of years later. Egyptologists have discovered that embalmers used honey in their preparations of mummifying their dead. Raw honey only changes when it gets cold. It crystalizes.

If your honey crystalizes, just put the jar in a pot of hot water. Never microwave your honey. It will zap the living stuff right out of it. Take the time and put it in warm water. If you heat the honey too much, you might as well have bought it from China.

It seems ridiculous to write about how to use your honey. Some people use it to make barbeque sauce and honey breads. We prefer to keep our honey uncooked and use it on top of fresh-baked bread or scones, though we do put it in our tea. By the time the tea is cool enough to drink, it won't affect the honey.

When you consider that one bee will produce 1/18th of a teaspoon of honey in her lifetime, you realize how precious every teaspoon is. When you make the commitment to keep bees (not exploit them), the value of your honey goes up even more.

Beekeepers have invested a lot of money and time in the keeping of bees. They feed their bees sugar when there is no nectar flow (late fall and winter) but never during the honey-producing times. Beekeepers pay attention to the health of their bees, feeding them protein and pollen when it is time for the queen to lay brood. They inspect their hives, treat for mites, and wrap them up for the winter. They always save enough honey for the bees to overwinter, using the sugar feed as an emergency food supply only.

When you buy local honey, you are supporting a local beekeeper who has committed money, time, and energy in a selfless manner. Most hives these days don't make it. What motivates small beekeepers is their commitment to the bees. That's how they can bring you honest-to-goodness honey.

22. VULNERABILITY
July 1, 2015

I have been feeling really vulnerable lately. I'm worried about what people think of me and I'm struggling with my ability to write. In fact, the last few months have been a constant struggle between my need to write and my need for privacy. The more excuses I make for keeping my words to myself to protect this privacy, the more conflicted I feel.

When friends ask, "How's the writing going?" I answer with some clever little excuse like, "I was getting too full of myself." And we laugh because that statement makes it true. I don't want to become full of myself. I don't want to try to appear as though I have any answers. The best I can say is that I think way too much about the questions.

There's a danger zone with this kind of writing. I know, I've heard every critical comment about one of the best known *journalists*, Henry David Thoreau (and he deserves them all- I'm sure he would agree). A word, once written, can so easily be attacked for its lack of integrity. By nature, what I write today will not be my truth three years from now.

And here's another thing: Mike and I have no intention of becoming the next Nearings. God bless them for everything they contributed to the human race. In fact, Mike and I owe much to them. If you're not sure who they are, look up *The Good Life*, and you'll know exactly what I mean.

The truth is, we don't feel as though we have anything special to teach people who would like to come up here and hang out with us, though we might have something to offer. I mean, we both love company and we both love to share. We just love spontaneity a lot more.

And truth be told, we are not doing anything someone else couldn't do better. We're making tons of mistakes and don't mind sharing them (except a couple of really ugly ones!).

One thing that journaling a real experience will do is expose a person to criticism. It's inevitable. It's the ultimate experience in vulnerability. It is, I am slowly learning, the best thing I can do to build inner fortitude. Vulnerability, I am discovering, is making me a much better person.

Being able to share my weaknesses with my kids, Mike, and my friends allows them the freedom to be fallible themselves. It's okay to be human. It's okay to not be okay sometimes. Honesty builds relationships you can depend on.

I have always hoped that my heart would provide a good place for my loved ones to land when they are falling. In order for me to do that, I must keep my heart strong and flexible. Most landings of that sort require a big heart for a landing pad. That means your heart needs to get a lot of exercise.

There's a serious part of me that argues if I expose my weaknesses to people, I'm giving them something to hold against me. This is true.

Some might accuse me of being irresponsible for suggesting people eat weeds indiscriminately or that I am encouraging people to go out and rake the environment clear of natural resources. I'm aware that my words could be misinterpreted. Some might say that I falsely paint a picture of being all alone in the woods. (I have neighbors now and I'm glad.)

"That's the danger of putting yourself out there," my friend W said. "There is such a thing as being too nice, you know," she adds with a cautionary tone. Also true. But keeping my experiences to myself or forcing myself to write fiction keeps me up at night. I'd rather be open and allow things to happen than keep waking up at all hours trying to resist my life's purpose.

It is so obvious to me when I am not following the path I am supposed to be taking. My body rebels and I carry around a headache the size of Vermont and just as land-locked. It's no good, I tell you. It's far better to be vulnerable.

Give me honest vulnerability and I know where we stand. When people posture and judge, I am completely thrown off. I don't feel like I can trust you if you try to be something. I'm sure I have been guilty of this myself on occasion but there's always some kind of churning in my gut when I am trying too hard that tells me to back off, breathe, and just be.

So, to be honest, I have been doing just about the opposite of what I set out to do two years ago. Lately, I have been running around, picking up whatever work I can get, eating a less than exemplary diet, and basically falling back into my old patterns of haste and waste. All of this has required more money, consequently requiring me to pick up more outside work. All the running around has depleted me physically, creatively, and spiritually.

It has proven far too easy to do. It has also kept me from my true purpose: to write.

And I feel it.

I also see it around me. Projects on the house have been slowing down, making our home an almost-finished place. Don't get me wrong. We have accomplished much in the last two years. But we also have reached a point where we can live in the house the way it is. That leaves you feeling as though you can't do anything fun because you've got so much still to do. It's a stale cycle because denying yourself the fun stuff robs you of valuable ambition: the true currency of efficiency.

Driving up to the house reminds you of what needs doing, like removing the excess wood and clutter from under the deck. Doing little things like taking a shower isn't relaxing because you are reminded that the tile work needs to be finished. It's not a pretty picture, I know. But it's true.

A cluttered, saw-dusty house makes you feel a little vulnerable when people come to visit. Your lack of ambition is right out there in plain sight. Your lack of organization and even cleanliness can be downright embarrassing if you look at it that way. And sometimes I do.

But then I remind myself that people don't really care about my housekeeping abilities (well, some might). The truth is they usually like my company for other reasons and know I'm not good at housekeeping anyway. A deeper truth is most people are busy worrying about what you're thinking of them to notice.

Then other times I think, "Yup, but look at what we **have** done." I'm not a best-selling author living in a perfect little dream home with a perfect husband and a perfect little life. That's just not me and I don't really want it to be.

The world I inhabit comes with my empty potato chip bags and Mike's plastic soda bottles in the back seat of the car. It also comes with a promise that soon, very soon, that soda will be replaced with homemade shrugs and tree teas. It also comes with the frustration of a wife that has to clear off the passenger seat of sharp tools and greasy lunch items just to get into the car.

It's a world that includes the smell of a mouse that made its way into the engine of the little old Honda. It's the sight of a clothes hanger bent into the shape of a heart to replace the antennae that broke off years ago and the dent a student driver left in the back panel.

It is, in short, a normal life inhabited by two humans who are lucky enough to have each other, kids, and family who have their own human lives.

I come to the conclusion that a life full of secrets is a truly vulnerable life. Perhaps real freedom isn't so much about being able to walk away from a complex life of myriad bills and scheduled vacation days. Maybe it has more to do with the ability to accept our own imperfections, admit them frankly to those who bear witness, and then let go with a chuckle and a shrug. No one can hold that against you.

Maybe the feeling of vulnerability comes more from avoidance. It could be that it comes from knowing that it's not feeling full of myself that keeps me from writing, it's feeling *devoid* of myself.

SHRUBS OR SHRUGS?

I'm not sure which name is correct, but like most things that are as old as this, it probably has had many names over the years and, well, it doesn't really matter, does it? This drink recipe has been around since the early Middle Ages and still makes perfect sense today as a way to pleasantly hydrate.

My friend Heather taught me how to make shrugs a few years ago and I have been making them ever since. There is a farm tradition that makes *switchell* which is the same recipe but includes molasses for added nutrition. *Switchell* was most often used during haying since it's pretty easy to get dehydrated and suffer heat stroke when you're gathering hay.

The recipe includes filling a glass canning jar half full with berries or herbs (or combinations of these) and then adding a sweetener of choice (it can be brown sugar, maple syrup, or honey) and then apple cider vinegar. Let it sit for about three weeks, shaking the jar occasionally to macerate the fruit. Some people let the sugar and herbs sit for a night in the refrigerator before adding the vinegar.

Add a couple of tablespoons to a glass of water and you have a refreshing drink any time of the year.

Vinegar will preserve the phytonutrients of the berries. It is good for your metabolism. It also can leech the calcium out of your teeth and bones if you drink too much of it so be mindful in your consumption. Like everything, balance is key.

23. DR. POTTS
August 13, 2015

While I haven't been writing much lately, I have been honoring the muse. The truth is, if I don't do something creative, I begin to feel as though I am wasting my life. It sounds weird but what most people consider a waste of time is exactly what I need to feel as though I'm doing something valuable. When life gets too hectic making money and spending it, I feel like it is spiraling out of control. Go figure.

Without creative projects, the muse nags at me in the middle of the night, tugging at the back of my neck, forcing a restlessness in my legs and feet. These movements won't let me sleep. That's when I usually wake up cranky and a little (sometimes a lot) hard to deal with.

That's why I make regular visits to Dr. Potts, my therapist and friend. My visits help me with the gap-times between writing. What is the prescription for feeling good and sleeping well again? One potter's wheel, two pounds of clay, a small bucket of water, and keeping my head down while I try to keep everything centered.

Clay makes pots; pots make me happy.

At first my pots were all wonky and misshapen. I could not, no matter how hard I tried, find the center. You can still make a bowl without centering the clay but it won't be symmetrical and it will be hard to get any height out of it. In short, everything you make will be …well, short.

Sometimes this might force new potters to get frustrated. What I have found is that everyone reacts differently to the challenge of a potter's wheel but anyone who sticks with it will eventually find the center.

Then, some days you just lose it and can't make anything useful, no matter how hard you try. If art is an expression of life, then pottery is the ultimate art.

When you go to a little fair in your town and you stop in to a potter's booth, you never realize how many pots that person threw away or gave away just to make that bowl or mug you hold in your hand.

My friend and mentor, Lyn, told me that in Japan, student potters are required to make 1,000 pots before they are allowed to keep one. That sounds like a lot. I think I may have lost count after the first 150 or so. In the beginning, I could not wait to see what my pots looked like. I couldn't wait to eat out of them or use them for morning coffee.

One of the problems is that it takes a while to make a pot you can actually eat out of. The truth is, it takes a long time to make a pot, even for experienced potters. If you work with a nice group of other potters, you either have to wait to collect enough pots to go into the kiln or you have to wait your turn because there are too many lined up. Firing the kiln takes a lot of time and energy so it doesn't happen unless there are enough pots to fill an entire kiln. If you are making pots to sell at festivals or for special orders, your pots go into the kiln first. It makes sense.

On top of that, every pot has to be fired twice: once for what is called bisque-firing, and then again to set the glaze. But before any firing can be done, the pot has to dry slowly or it will crack, and you have to put your pot back on the wheel to trim off any clay that isn't necessary.

Let's just say there are a lot of steps to making a pot. Each step has its perils. So, if you do manage to center everything (which as we already discussed, doesn't always happen), and you manage to get the pot off the wheel without any incident, you cover it well enough so it dries slowly so there are no cracks, and you get it to the point when you can trim off excess clay, it can go horribly wrong if you miscalculate how much clay to remove when you trim it on the wheel and you tear a hole right through your piece.

There are times when you think it might be wise to just give up. That's when your buddy arrives and says something funny like, "Wow! You're still at it, huh?"

And you think, "Yah, why **am** I still at it? Maybe I should just stick to what I'm good at. What *was* that again?" Blah, blah, blah…

That happened the day that there was a fly that made its way into the studio and it kept buzzing in my ear and landing on my face. It was driving me crazy as I swiped at it with clay-covered hands. I was getting clay all over my face and couldn't concentrate on the center of the wheel so I just scooped up the clay, threw it in a little bucket with other wet clay that didn't do my bidding that day, and washed up.

That was also the day I decided to find out what the fly was trying to tell me. Usually, I have a few books on animal symbolism that help me identify characteristics of what message certain animals might be bringing to me. That day I decided to just google it on my phone and had to laugh when I read what my sources all said.

"So, it says here that the fly is about persistence," I tell Lyn.

Lyn has come to accept my goofiness so stuff like talking about animal symbolism doesn't surprise her. And anyway, who could argue with the clarity of that message? She smiled in affirmation. If anyone understands the importance of persistence, it's a potter.

I went back to the wheel. "Yes, I'm still at it. *Yes.*"

I have come to the conclusion that if I never am able to make a centered pot that I would be proud to sell at a festival, I will have gained something more important. Dr. Potts will have taught me that above all else, there is power in persistence.

I have come to the conclusion that I will have to create a lot of little, funky pots on my journey. I have learned that being good at something is more about experience than it is about trying to be perfect.

My sessions with Dr. Potts have taught me to be grateful for my own quirky imperfections. The wonkiness makes my pots different and fun. My pottery friends have dubbed my creations "happy pots" because they make people smile. I **am** happy when I make them because I am not obsessed with perfection. I know it's not something I can achieve yet. I have learned that it is the imperfections that make my pots fun. I am learning to laugh at the lines that don't connect or the little splashes of glaze that ended up where I did not plan.

Recently, I decided that I will not try to draw a straight line. I decreed: *All lines will be crooked.* I think that will look cool on a perfectly centered large bowl someday.

PITFIRING POTTERY

A lot of people think you need expensive equipment to make pottery but that isn't necessarily true. My friends and I have been on a quest for making pottery that is relatively strong, will hold water, is non-toxic, and that you can fire in your backyard.

What we discovered is that there are many ways to do such a thing. In fact, people all over the world are still making functional pottery without an electric kiln or even a lot of firewood or other fuels. I have only tried pit firing but the results have been good. So far, the only pot that broke in the pit was the pot I stepped on by accident when I was placing them in. The method I will describe to you is something that most people can accomplish if they have access to some scrap wood and a somewhat open space.

Making the pots requires that you use a clay that has a fair amount (about twenty percent, we estimate) of what is called *grog* in the clay. An easy way to do this is to purchase a terracotta clay already mixed. We have used a sandy clay from a friend's yard that worked very well for small items with thick walls. We have also used stoneware clay with ground-up already-fired pots kneaded in and other clays that are grainy. If they are too smooth, they will crack because the moisture from the pot builds up and can't escape without the little openings that the grit provides. The steam that builds up in the walls of the pots will create their own openings, if you don't plan correctly.

Clay is an exact science and can get a little daunting when you start to read about it but try not to let it stop you from doing it. Try different methods and see how they turn out. The members of your group have to be willing to accept the fact that your experiment might not work. But if they make several pieces using different clays, the probability that they will walk away with a pot will increase.

Methods for hand-building a pot vary greatly. If you use coils, make sure the coils are connected well by smoothing out the surface of the pot with you fingers as you build the walls. Also, start with a smooth disk you have rolled out for the bottom, not coils because once your coil pot is made, you won't be able to lift it to smooth out the bottom coils. I know, I tried it the other way.

You can also roll out slabs and make your cups and plates by seaming pieces together. Score each surface and use a little water to attach pieces. Let those pots dry slowly. If it is winter or if your region is arid, cover the pots with plastic bags so they don't crack. Keep an eye on them and layer the plastic if they are drying too fast.

When you can pick your pot up without changing its shape, burnish it with a smooth stone, your finger, the back of a spoon, or (my preferred method) a plastic bag wrapped around your finger. You can apply a little water under each patch that you work. You can also use oil which can create a lovely metallic effect when it carbonizes. We have used bear fat to make our pots impermeable to water. Burnishing strengthens the pots and makes them waterproof.

Make sure your pots are bone dry before you fire them. You can put them in a 250 degree oven before the firing to make sure the temperature of the pot doesn't change drastically before placing them in the pit. We have done this and it works fine (so far).

Dig a pit about three feet deep and four feet wide. If you have a lot of pots, make your pit a little wider. Layer in a little wood (doesn't have to be hardwood- we used construction debris from our house and it worked fine), add a one-foot deep layer of sawdust, cow dung (if you have access to it), pots nestled in, dung, sawdust, a layer of pottery chards or something that will act as a heat reflector but allows air to circulate, and then kindling and wood on top. Light the fire and add wood for about two to three hours. Let the wood burn really hot and when you have mostly coals going, cover the pit with scraps of metal roofing. Seal the edges with dirt. Let it smolder for three days. It has to be completely cool before you open it up.

A couple of key things to remember are to make sure when you take the chunks of grassy sod out as you begin to dig the ditch, turn them upside-down so the grass is protected. You'll be glad you did this when you fill the pit at the end. The grass will be happy you did this too. Count your pieces before placing them in the pit and place smaller items inside bigger ones so that they are easier to find. It is okay for pots to touch each other.

Opening the pit is a lot like a treasure hunt. There is an indescribable sense of community anticipation when you unveil the pit. But digging the clay, making the pots, burnishing them, and digging the pit, collecting the dung, and gathering the wood are also wonderful events for any group of people. Creativity on a community level creates a magical bond between people that few other things can. Creating a pot in your backyard that you can use for your morning oatmeal, well, that's hard to beat!

24. ETHER
August 28, 2015

In *Walking Away*, I wrote about the power of faith from my own experience. I guess what I have discovered since then is that faith is an ongoing process that changes as we grow. I have also discovered that it cannot accurately be labeled as anything other than individual to a person. My view of what I have faith in doesn't completely fit anyone else's. I think of it more as a twinkle in a person's eye.

I am not an Animist, Spiritualist, Christianist, Buddhist, Shamanist, Alchemist, Taoist, or Traditionalist. In fact, I don't think any *"ist"* can define what I believe.

The other day while driving to Caribou on an invitation to attend a Micmac powwow, Mike pondered, "If a person believes in an all-powerful God, then why wouldn't that person believe that He would send messages through whatever means works? That could mean messages from heart-shaped rocks, words in the clouds, animal visits, dreams; whatever that person can relate to."

That right there is another solid reason to appreciate Mike. In one breath he'll say how much he disdains the "Coexist" bumper sticker popular right now. The word is written in different religious symbols. In the next breath, he'll express his agreement with the concept. I guess what Mike appreciates most is being an individual and expressing original ideas. Bumper stickers are the antithesis of individualism.

While at the powwow, Mike and I talked at length with Jerry White Elk. He was jovial and friendly the whole weekend until he asked me this question, "Are you one of those Wiccans or something?" His tone was a little serious all of a sudden, "Because my people don't like that."

My answer was probably a little more forceful than I would have planned.

"I don't like to be labeled anything."

"Well, you seem to lean in that direction…"

"The only thing I can say about what I believe is that I am a child of God and ask every day to be of service to His love and light. Whatever that makes me, then yes, I am that!"

Jerry seemed to like my answer. I have no idea if all who are Wiccan believe in the tenet, "harm none." My guess is they will only practice good things, unless they want to fall prey to their own harmful intentions.

What we put forth in life is what ends up surrounding us and I'm pretty sure they understand that. What goes around, comes around. It's the Golden Rule of thumb: don't do anything to anyone you wouldn't want done to you because all actions cause a reaction, or something like that. What Jerry finds egregious, he explained, is when people want to wield power over others. I agree with him on all levels. I avoid those types myself.

As far as only doing the absolute peaceful and loving thing at all times, I don't think I really am Christian enough to say I could do that. If I am attacked, I will respond as best as I can to halt my attacker using whatever means available to me, including deadly force.

I believe in forgiveness, and understand that it is more about being able to travel lightly when we walk away from bad situations. Turning the other cheek, however, doesn't make enough practical sense to me yet. I am willing to defend another person's right to respond that way to an attacker and fully appreciate the higher road that person has taken. Neither responding with force or peaceful resistance are easy routes.

When it comes to my own world view, I am also willing to discuss the benefits of following a purely Christian life according to The New Testament and Christ's teachings. But I'm more likely to think of Maya Angelou's answer to a woman who claimed to be a Christian. According to accounts, the author responded, "Already?!"

If you really think about it, it would take a lifetime to claim any one of these faiths. My answer is, "I'm not sure it's required of me anyway. I think what's required is to do my best to love my neighbor and myself. If someone is unlovable, I let God be the judge if I can't be loving."

As far as getting messages from rocks and animals like an Animist would, I plead guilty quite often. I have a deep understanding that reality can be transformed by our own thoughts, as an Alchemist believes and science is now proving. I seek the power of neutrality and the *middle way* like a Buddhist. I believe in the power and the beauty of Jesus as a God-man who taught us that God is in all of us even if we don't think so. And yet, I have no "*ist*" to call my own. If that separates me from some, and unites me with others, it makes no difference, because I am not afraid to stand alone in my faith.

It seems that this is the very reason so many Europeans (and my guess is, pre-Europeans) came to this land. Like me, a lot of people want to feel free to believe what gives them strength as long as it doesn't hurt anyone else.

Throughout history, people have been forced to give up their belief in rocks and plants and sky as the language of God. People have been beaten, burned, and buried alive for having the audacity to be an individual. It's really no laughing matter.

When I think of what it means to be an American, I think it has more to do with the freedom to hold individual beliefs and be able to talk and write about them. This may seem idealistic. It is. What makes it practical is respect and law. Our Founding Fathers knew enough about history and human nature to write the Bill of Rights and the first of those constitutional laws is the First Amendment.

Granting that whatever a person thinks is between that person and his Maker is all about respect. I don't need to have faith in your beliefs in order to have faith that it will help you. I also have faith in the law that allows you to practice what you wish as long as it doesn't harm me or others.

I say power and faith are uncomfortable bed fellows.

Jerry says that faith and power can never be bedfellows. Since, he says, they are truly two altogether different concepts.

"If you have faith," he told Mike and me, "you are asking the Creator to *show* you."

"I am talking with Him but I'm showing Him the respect He deserves. If you search to use power over others, you've lost before you start because it is no longer you controlling it. It is controlling you," Jerry explained.

This is why I think faith should be personal. I'm not suggesting people stop meeting and looking for guidance, whether in church or temple, or around a fire. I love to circle-up and worship. It gives me strength. But keeping faith personal gives individuals the power to decide who holds power over them. Faith in a higher power gives people the ability to look beyond another human (or group of humans) who may wish to wield harm and see that other people hold no power over them. That's why governments so often try to control a people's faith.

Recently, Pope Francis spoke to the people of Cuba. He met with Raul and Fidel Castro (who might want to make peace with the Creator before expiring, just saying). The remarkable thing to me is that so many people showed up to practice mass with the Pope. I think this indicates that since the 1960's, when the people of Cuba were forbidden to practice their faith, they still held on to something more powerful than their government. I imagine they must have felt pretty relieved to be able to finally worship in public.

I used to know an old man in Miami Beach who would stand on the edge of the island every day gazing in the direction of Cuba. He had been held prisoner for close to twenty years because he was vocal about his faith. That man looked a lot older than he was for a reason. (No joke here.)

What I liked about this old man is, in spite of his traumatic experience, he was happy to routinely share fruits from his ten-foot square garden with a young mother passing by with a baby carriage. He had cultivated his garden. However tiny in size, his garden in Miami Beach was replete with tropical fruits, herbs, and vegetables.

Though I appreciated the fruits and gardening advice he shared with me, the best part about this man, I always thought, is that he had a twinkle in his eye and a radiant smile.

To me, that is the power of faith.

THE HOLLOW BONE

Native American healers and elders practice *Being the Hollow Bone.* It is a concept that I have encountered in other healing practices as well.

Simply put, *being the hollow bone* is consciously putting aside one's own thoughts, doubts, and judgements (some might call it *the ego-self*), and allowing the higher powers to work through the practitioner's words and actions. I'm pretty sure that is what my great-grandmother was doing when she practiced her Christian Science faith healing.

A simple intention or prayer opens the avenue for the higher powers to work. These prayers most often request that only benevolence be allowed to transpire. The intention is always that whatever comes through this cleared out space is an agent for the greater good of all concerned.

In yoga, we think of tuning ourselves like a flute-maker would tune a flute. Then we set the intention that we remain clear of any obstruction that might impede the clear sound of a beautiful melody that plays through us. Zen Buddhists will meditate to invite a void in the dwelling-place of the mind. An artist will clear the way for inspiration to come through. They may refer to the Muse.

I believe that it is all the same thing. My friends who regularly practice Reiki (and other energy-based healing) begin their practices with the same intentions. Clearing oneself out of the way is an important ritual. But, calling it a ritual makes it sound really mechanical and it is anything but mechanical and routine.

I believe all artists, writers, healers, holy men and women, (including more orthodox clergy) practice this. Christians will call on Jesus to guide their efforts and work through them. Like any practice, *the hollow bone* becomes clearer with exercise and training.

I believe that those who sincerely ask a benevolent Higher Power to guide them to serve others are engaged in this practice.

It is a powerful medicine since healers need healing too. It is a recognition that any power we have comes from a higher source: the Creator of all. We can only be great when we allow that force to work through us. The way I see it, you know it's there when you see a twinkle in someone's eye.

25. TIME
October 11, 2015

Last Saturday afternoon, we got some really sad news. Pastor Isaiah's house burned down. The fire started in the barn and spread so fast that everything went. The good news is that it was daytime and the pastor and his wife got out in time so no one was hurt. The news station sent out a helicopter and we could see pictures of the damages on Mike's phone.

That's why, on our way into the neighboring town to pick up some car parts, dressed in well-oiled coveralls and clay-stained jeans, we decided to stop in at the church and ask what was being done to help the Pastor and his wife. It was ten o'clock on a Sunday and we knew there would be somebody in the church at that time. We wanted to know how we could help.

As we entered the church and peered through the windows of the inner sanctuary doors, we saw the pastor, all clean in a new pair of slacks and a crisp green shirt with coordinating tie. He was talking to a tall gentleman in a grey suit.

"Maybe we shouldn't go in. I'm dressed for mechanic work, not church." *Yes*, I thought, *that car definitely has him on his knees today! No worries, God doesn't care what you look like when you show up.* I opened the door.

"Hi Pastor. We are so sorry about your loss. We were just passing by and wanted to know what we could do to help out."

His smile said it all.

"Yes, I guess those rutabagas are cooked about now," he joked.

As he told us about the fire and that his insurance company had just cancelled on them a month ago, Isaiah's smile never left his face. In his retelling of things, his focus was on how people had been helping. He pointed to his new clothes and gestured over to his wife and told us how wonderful she is and what a lucky man he has been.

"You know what you can do for me, friends? You have already done it. You are here."

We knew we had to get to the car parts store before it closed so I was thinking, *Well, maybe next Sunday, Pastor. We're hardly dressed for church and we have errands to run this morning.*

Mike looked at me. The pastor looked at me. He wasn't pressuring us to stay for the sermon. He was just happy that we had stopped in.

"We have something we have to do in town. We'll be back in half an hour. Is it okay if we're a little late?" Mike had already read the situation and knew what was important.

What the Pastor needed from us was to just spend a little time in prayer with him. In Isaiah's case, prayer means singing and celebrating the Good News that he has to share. His faith that everything will be alright keeps the smile on his face but is amplified by the people who show up and sit in the pews.

As Mike once commented, we don't need "Two or more to gather in His name…" God is always present. I think what we really need is to look into each other's eyes and see God reflected there in their love for us. I think that's what the Biblical verse means. When we gather together, we share His love for us.

All Isaiah wanted from us at that moment was to join him in a song. It took one hour out of our day but it was time well-spent. Nevertheless, I think he would have been just as content to see the love in our eyes when we walked into his church to see him.

In exchange, we had the privilege of witnessing how Isaiah and his wife, two people of faith, deal with adversity. We got to take a tour through the Bible and all of the different stories about how people have always had their share of difficulties, but God did provide.

I got to keep the imprint of Isaiah's smile beaming out of his crisp green shirt. His faith is authentic and I feel very comfortable in his presence. His gaze doesn't ask me to make any kind of commitment. It is loving and speaks to me of gratitude.

"Someone asked me if I'm not sad I lost everything," he said. "I told them I wasn't planning on taking that house with me when I go." Somehow, coming from him, that statement didn't sound cliché at all.

When Mike and I left, we said to each other, "All he wanted from us was our time. It is amazing that only one day after absolutely everything he owns is incinerated, he is still smiling."

Helping Isaiah cost us nothing but our time.

Time, it turns out, is the one thing we are free to give. Mike pointed out recently that it is the one thing you give that you can never get back. It's the ultimate in the department store gift department.

I guess if I can say anything about our decision to move off grid and get control of our expenditures, it's that it gives us sovereignty over our time. We are just as busy as ever but if a friend or family member needs us (NOW), we are free to go.

When we budget out our resources, Mike and I admit that money is not a strong one. We count family, friends, our experience and work ethic, food, shelter, and our time as our primary resources. Money will always be short and, like Isaiah pointed out so pertinently, you can't take it with you.

Things, even things like shelter, and people, even family, can change. The cars we drive and all the stuff we need are all just junk eventually. But what we choose to do with the time we have been given is something we do have. Whether it is short or long, our time is precious and our sovereignty over it is even more so.

A SOLAR-POWERED LIFE

I once met a man while I was traveling in Guatemala who told me the sun is a god. He said, "It is the only thing that never changes. It is the only thing we can depend on and it gives us light and warmth, two things all living beings absolutely need to survive."

I couldn't argue with his reasoning. I know I sure do appreciate the sun. These days, I pay a lot of attention to it. I am also fully grateful for its power and our ability to harness that power.

It took a little while to shift to an off-grid lifestyle. But patience pays off when we stop to consider that, other than taxes and insurance, we have no fixed bills. All other expenses are things we can control like food, gas, propane, and other necessities. We heat with wood and try to keep our needs simple.

Aside from the comment, "Wow! I can't believe how well I slept last night," the next most common remark we get is, "Wait, this house is off-grid? It doesn't seem like it."

That's probably because we might have music playing, lights on, vacuumed rugs (most of the time), running water, and any other convenience necessary.

When Mike and I started planning this lifestyle seven years ago, we knew that powering our house with a solar array would be one of our larger expenses. We were prepared to wait until we could afford it. In the meantime, we would use the small solar power systems that can be purchased in most box stores now. We knew that every year solar power would be more economical and the quality would improve. We were right.

We didn't realize how rapidly the technology would improve and become cost-effective. In a matter of a few months of living in our new house, we were able to afford solar power. Like anything, the cost is more about installation than equipment so if you are willing to learn a lot really fast, you can make it happen too.

Mike installed all of the outlets and wiring in our house. The solar array was set up by a professional (Lee Solar) who also checked the wiring to make sure it was done right. Like most of the people who have done work for us, he eventually became a good friend.

The main thing to remember about a solar system is the panels are set up in sequences so if you start with three, you have to add another three if you want to expand. You will also want to familiarize yourself with terms like *sine wave inverter*. It is also important to plan ahead based on the lifestyle you plan to enjoy. Things like owning a television mean nothing to us so we didn't plan for it.

You'll also have to secure a dry place for the batteries. We have twelve deep cycle batteries that need to be checked once a month for water level. Eventually we will have to replace batteries, but our plan is to add to them slowly so it is not one big expense all at once. Once you get the hang of it, solar is a very efficient and cost-effective way to bring light and comfort to your world.

I can use any electronic gadget I would like, including my bread machine, dehydrator, vacuum cleaner, washing machine, food blender, yoghurt maker, food processor, and kitchen aid.

We do have to be a little careful with our usage in the winter but last winter we only used our generator once. (It was a pretty long winter too!) I don't need the bread maker or the yoghurt maker in the winter. I can proof everything on the back of the wood stove or in my new proofing oven.

Coordinating when you accomplish some chores becomes an art form when you live off-grid. Our biggest draw on the system is our well. To offset this draw we purchased a larger water tank and installed a soft-start well pump. But we do have to watch water usage when people come to visit. Things like flushing the toilet less often are just a part of the adjustments when you live off-grid. I have also resurrected Grandma's dishwashing method of using a sink full of soapy water and filling the other sink with clean rinse water instead of letting the water run. I have learned to schedule things like laundry and vacuuming for sunny days.

From a positive perspective, it encourages us to be mindful of our use of water. It also limits our bread intake and gets me up early on a sunny day to maximize my washing and cleaning time. All-in-all, it is a healthy way to live, I say.

It also makes me feel cognizant and grateful for every drop of sun that comes my way.

EPILOGUE
October 10, 2015

This summer I have been busy canning up everything in sight. Mike worked for a contractor friend who had been looking for someone with experience. Because of that job, we were able to save up the money we needed for materials to build our woodshed and to seal the house.

We figure that these two items were the last of our serious construction costs. From here on out, it is maintenance and finishing touches like closets and indoor trim on the doors. We have been creative about our interior window trim, using live-edged pine we "bought" from a friend who owns a saw mill. We traded honey for the boards and now our window sills look like they belong in a Log Home magazine. Our friend threw in a heavy slab of oak that I sanded and coated several times with polyurethane and Mike made a coffee table with it.

We are busy. But it reminds me that you take yourself wherever you go. When we sit in that *bored room* meeting and our minds wander to that last time we were out in nature. The *you* in that meeting is not the only *you*. There's a wilderness in us that knows it would do just fine "out there." It's the *one* that knows that we don't need the *bored room meeting* world, **it needs us.**

Mike and I remember when someone asked us some time back, "What will you do out there?"

We laugh because we are just as busy as we ever were, maybe more. Today we will be volunteering our morning to fix up the old grange hall in our town of 212 residents. My friend Lyn will be bringing zucchini bread and I'll be bringing zucchini marmalade I recently set up. It's a pretty green color and something new.

Later on we were invited to set up a lunch and skills share for through-hikers on the Appalachian Trail. Our friend Sam is organizing it and we talked about it at a Fourth of July Party. We're not sure we'll make it, but would like to.

I have been substitute-teaching: a constant reminder that I have so much more to learn. I also have spent some time becoming a better potter and developing my own style that reflects my Caribbean heritage and a joyful attitude. I teach three yoga classes a week and am happy to be providing a good service to the people in my area. Yoga is something I am enthusiastic about and people seem to like its gentle, yet effective, approach to health. It keeps me healthy too.

Mike has been doing something he has always wanted to do; he is learning how to build houses. (Which is something, he says, you should always do after you build your own house.) He is very happy, though he leaves the house before six every morning. He also has been coaching fast pitch softball. He tutors pitchers and catchers three or four nights a week and has developed a stellar reputation in our area.

We are both content being valuable members of our community. We have volunteered, traded, and worked our way to being of service and it has provided us with enough.

We feel more alive than ever because we are learning. We are busy making use of every minute and every opportunity. This requires being creative and knowing what to do with things that other people might not want or need, like making zucchinis into marmalade.

Since I began writing my *Waking up from the American Dream* series, I have become comfortable with climbing ladders (sometimes with a cup of coffee in each hand!), hammering nails, and thinking through construction decisions with Mike and others. Now I am just as interested in talking about building as I am about discussing the right pair of boots that can go from office to trail climbing in one day.

I am learning how to be strong in my vulnerability and some of my earlier convictions have changed. In spite of my assertions about going gray, I eventually gave in to my cousins' pressure to highlight my hair again. I'm happy they convinced me to do it. It's okay to change your mind.

I have grown in other ways too. I suppose the continued exposure to all of the silence has contributed to a type of growth I had not anticipated. I knew building a house and living off-grid would make me stronger in body and mind. What I had not considered was what it would do to my spirit.

I guess I have begun to realize that slow and steady does win the race (if life were a race, **and it isn't**). I think we all reach that understanding, at some point, sometime. We conclude that those who have joined us as we travel through life were never competitors, even the ones who thought they were. They were always just gifts.

Maybe I needed all of this solitude to truly appreciate all of the gifts I have been given. Each person who has shared the road with me at various times has taught me something about myself that I needed to learn. For that I am truly grateful. This realization has provided me with a kind of peace and I am glad to be in its presence.

There is some other transformation that is occurring in me that is guiding my writing as I work on Book III of this series. It is an awakening of a deeper part of me that I have begun allowing myself to share. As I grow, I move through the fear of forging my own path through the woods of life. Using my heart as my compass, I know I'll find my way.

The process of trusting in my life's purpose has taken me some time. There are those who know what they must do from the beginning of their lives. They act on that knowledge and never waiver, no matter the difficulty. If life were a race, I suppose those would be the ribbon-holders and they deserve the accolades.

If you think about it, it's all about trust. Writing *Walking Away* taught me to trust in my life's purpose. Writing *Making it Home* has taught me to trust in the process and see how my writing serves others.

Writing Book III, *Keeping it Real*, is teaching me to trust in a Higher Power and to seek this greater authority in me. It is the part of me that sees beyond ego or personality and gives me courage. I need fear nothing.

It is exciting to follow my own path through the woods. Getting off the paved road is where the true treasures lie. Though sometimes, I might get a little lost, my heart is my compass.

I am making it home.

BIBLIOGRAPHY

The following is a list of resources that Mike and I have used. I tried to include any authors to whom I refer in my books. The Digital Age offers ready access to most of these resources. I made a strong attempt to refer to these resources in such a manner that anyone could execute an easy Internet search for more information or to check the validity of my sources.

Akkermans, Anthonnio. Bushcraft Skills and How to Survive in the Wild: A Step-by-Step Practical Guide. London; Annes Publishing, Ltd., 2007

Audobon Birds, Wildflowers, Mushrooms

Bennett, Chris. Southeast Foraging: 120 wild and flavorful edibles from angelica to wild plum. London; Timber Press, 2015

Conrad, Ross. Natural Beekeeping: Oragnic Approaches to Modern Apiculture. Vermont; Chelsea Green Publishing, 2007

Farmer, Steven D. Animal Spirit Guides. New York; Hay House, Inc., 2006

Gehring,Abigail R. Back to Basics. New York; Skyhorse Publishing, 2008

Gehring, Abigail R. The Homesteading Handbook. New York; Skyhorse Publishing, 2011

Green, James. The Herbal Medicine-Maker's Handbook, A Home Manual. Berkeley, CA; Crossing Press, 2000

Haines, Arthur. Ancestral Plants, A Primitive Skills Guide to Important Edible, Medicinal, and Useful Plants of the Northeast, Volumes 1 and 2. Maine; Anaskimin Publishing, 2015

Hubbell, Sue. <u>A Book of Bees</u>. Boston; Houghton Mifflin Company, 1988

Kallas, John. <u>Edible Wild Plants: Wild Foods from Dirt to Plate</u>. Utah; Gibbs Smith, 2010

Kloss, Jethro. <u>Back to Eden</u>. Wisconsin; Lotus Press, 1939

Lincoff, Gary. <u>The Complete Mushroom Hunter: An Illustrated Guide to Finding, Harvesting, and Enjoying Wild Mushrooms</u>. Beverly, MA; Quarry Books, 2010

Peterson, Roger Tory and McKenny, Margaret. <u>Peterson Field Guides: Wildflowers</u>. Boston; Houghton Mifflin, 1968

Peterson, Roger Tory and McKenny, Margaret. <u>Peterson Field Guides: Edible Wild Plants</u>. Boston; Houghton Mifflin, 1978

<u>National Audubon Society Field Guides to Northern American Mushrooms and Field Guide to Northern American Wildflowers</u>. New York; Alfred A. Knopf under Random House Publishers, 1981

Nearing, Helen and Scott. <u>The Good Life</u>. New York; Schocken Books Inc., 1970

Richardson, Joan. <u>Wild Edible Plants of New England: A Field Guide</u>. Yarmouth, ME; DeLorme Publishing Company, 1981

Sams, Jamie and Carson, David. <u>Medicine Cards: The Discovery of Power through the Ways of Animals</u>. New York; St. Martin's Press, 1988

Schwab, Alexander. <u>Mushrooming Without Fear</u>. New York; Skyhorse Publishing, 2007

Thayer, Samuel. <u>Nature's Garden: A Guide to Identifying, Harvesting, and Preparing Edible Wild Plants</u>. Birchwood, WI; Forager's Harvest, 2010

Thoreau, Henry David. <u>Walden; Or, Life in the Woods</u>. New York; Dover Publications, 1995 (Originally published in 1854.)

Voltaire. <u>Candide</u>. New York; Dover Publications, 1991
(Originally published in 1759.)

Michele Maingot Cabral spent her formative years climbing trees with pocket knives and notebooks in the United States and the West Indies. Her interest in writing journals and poetry continued into adulthood. For close to two decades, she held a career as a Nationally Board Certified high school English teacher and holds a Masters in English Education.

She now lives with her husband Mike and their dog Hermes in an almost-completed off-grid cabin they built together in the woods of Maine. She writes, teaches yoga, substitute-teaches, swings a hammer, keeps bees, and forages for a living. She and Mike also created a line of salves and soaps that they sell locally.

She is the author of two books (*Walking Away* and *Making it Home*) in the series, *Waking up from the American Dream. S*he is presently working on Book III of that four-part series entitled, *Keeping it Real.*

Made in the USA
Charleston, SC
06 April 2016